AGELESS SPIRIT

By the same author

A second book about Ageless Spirit and the Inner Journey is to be published shortly—this time presented as a magic story for children, aged 10-100: *Edrin's Quest: Journey of a Soul.*

More information at www.diadembooks.com/lewis.htm

AGELESS SPIRIT

✦

Source of Joy, Strength, Creativity in Later Years

Dorothy Lewis

iUniverse, Inc.
New York Lincoln Shanghai

AGELESS SPIRIT
Source of Joy, Strength, Creativity in Later Years

Copyright © 2006 by Dorothy Lewis

iUniverse books may be ordered through booksellers or by contacting:

iUniverse
2021 Pine Lake Road, Suite 100
Lincoln, NE 68512
www.iuniverse.com
1-800-Authors (1-800-288-4677)

ISBN-13: 978-0-595-39792-1 (pbk)
ISBN-13: 978-0-595-84199-8 (ebk)
ISBN-10: 0-595-39792-1 (pbk)
ISBN-10: 0-595-84199-6 (ebk)

Printed in the United States of America

Contents

INTRODUCTION vii

Chapter 1   MAGIC 1

Chapter 2   COMMUNICATION 11

Chapter 3   ENERGIES 25

Chapter 4   RELATIONSHIPS 41

Chapter 5   ANGELS 59

Chapter 6   DEATH—The Approach 72

Chapter 7   DEATH—The Celebration 84

Chapter 8   HEALING 98

Chapter 9   DAMS and DITCHES 119

Chapter 10   STILLNESS 132

INTRODUCTION

Life can be seen from many angles, at its many different stages. Concepts change as we experience and grow. In this book we are exploring the time when we are older—Senior Citizen, OAP., or just 'not quite so young'. As someone in the late seventies, I share many of your feelings about old age. In fact, I personally have found this the most challenging period of my life. All the niggling old age changes, not quite so mobile, not quite so in the middle of things, not quite so agile and, horrors, not quite so useful; by contrast, more easily tired, more easily not quite so well, more easily feeling deserted, or lonely, or inadequate. And where do friends and relations go? Some move into homes, some travel to live with children, and, far too frequently it seems, some die.

So how do you, do I, cope with all this? I am absolutely awestruck sometimes at the vast courage shown by older people. They plod on, determinedly bright and cheerful, quite successfully disguising the depression, worry, even despair, hidden behind their stout front door. I often wonder, when someone asks, 'How are you?' and the automatic answer is 'Fine', how the questioner would react if you answered truthfully, in detail? Ouch!

But this book is absolutely not about these aspects of old age. For what are they but descriptions of the outer human shell? Shell, yes—not the real you at all. Who are you? I will tell you—you are Ageless Spirit. Part of the great Life/Love energy that encompasses and flows through every single life form—a huge, wonderful unifying energy. Ageless Spirit is tireless, is never ill or sad or defeated. It is magic and mystery and wonder, yet it can be expressed in as tiny a way as in the rescue of a wee fledgling that has fallen out of its nest and needs reuniting with its mother.

I'm sharing here some of the ways that we, older folk, can be in touch with our inner Ageless Spirit; can use magic, meet angels, share healing; and, best of all, can usefully, powerfully, spread in the world the so badly needed Ageless Spirit energy.

Good news. Enjoy it.

1

MAGIC

Why have I started with magic? Magic? In old age? One of the greatest traps in old age can be the attitude of 'shut down', 'That's over', 'I can't do that anymore', 'I shall never see him/her again', 'I can't drive the car much longer…' Not all the time, not everybody, but I suggest that as you read this you will recognise in yourself at least some of this attitude creeping in. Dealt with very differently, no doubt. Those with money may embark on convoluted holiday trips 'while we can'. Others splash out on more luxury material comforts, and so on. Could the real motive there be an attempt to put off the evil day—when they will have to stop running? And already many do decide on dogged acceptance, with enormous courage and an outward show of good humour and happiness.

And I want to blitz this constrictive approach, blow it up, send it away, change things. How? By using magic, life magic, soul magic, Ageless Spirit magic—available to us all if we choose to use it. So let's jump in the deep-end and have a look.

What does 'magic' mean to you? The Chambers dictionary gives a lovely definition: 'the art of producing marvellous results…by using the secret forces of nature.' This is such a beautifully open definition, resting on each person's interpretation of those 'secret forces'.

But it goes on to include 'sorcery', 'art of producing results by legerdemain (trickery)'. So on the one side you get the enormously popular Harry Potter books, on the other side dismissal: 'He's a charlatan,' 'it's just coincidence', 'more New Age rubbish, fantasy, make-believe.' Yet people seem to need magic of some sort. I feel that for those of us on the inner journey, to experience magic is to allow the Ageless Spirit to shine consciously in our lives, perhaps fleetingly, but with an unforgettable input and reassurance. Reality is there; to catch even a glimpse sets us back on track.

This is life magic. It is not made up of wizards and monsters, stories of danger and miraculous escapes. It can be recognised instead as a Quiet presence, breaking through into our outer everyday lives, sometimes in very unexpected places and times. Sometimes, too, in wonderfully down-to-earth ways.

Because isn't magic just something we can't understand? A minor miracle that never ceases to amaze me is the simple act of car-parking. As I leave home I always in my mind set up a parking space in the crowded market town, ten miles away. Reaching the town I find cars circling round, space-hunting. But as I drive round a car pulls out of 'my' space. This week I tried a new venture. Darlington, fine day, half term holiday, the town all hustle and bustle, and I wanted to go to my favourite 'caf' for a lunch snack. Impossible, but a thought came into my mind: 'Set it up, a place by the window.' As I came down the street I could see the 'caf' was crowded, no space anywhere—silly idea. But before I could back out I was beckoned by a woman, sitting on her own, in a place by the window! Coincidence? Of course.

Except that I no longer believe in coincidence. I don't pretend to understand how it works, but somehow energies flow and cross, very often unconscious energies, or energies more delicate than you can imagine. I am thinking of someone I haven't contacted for months, five minutes later the phone rings: 'Haven't heard from you lately, how are you?' Or I go into town for a specific purpose and just by chance go into a discount bookshop to fill in a few minutes. There is the book I've been seeking for months, and at less than half price. You can all give countless examples.

Which brings me to another fairly recent discovery. It's OK not to understand! My childhood education was totally messed up by the war and not until my own children were of school age could I venture forth, train as a teacher, then become a lecturer and finally embark on an M.Ed. degree, based on philosophy of education. There I had a wonderful tutor, very peaceful and kind, but ruthless in his eradication of surplus material. My first essays were riddled with remarks in tiny red writing: 'This is not clear.' 'What exactly does this mean?' 'I do not understand.' Complete untruth, he knew exactly what I meant, but that was not good enough. 'Say it exactly.' It was a great day when I had an essay returned with only one red remark: 'Good.'

So understanding meant clarity, at brain level, of course. Yet a couple of years later life threw me into the broadly liberal, sometimes apparently unstructured methods of the holistic approach to health. No, the holistic approach to human beings, to life. As a practitioner of complementary medicine, intuition became a valuable tool. Healing energies, to my unbelieving amazement, could be channelled with measurable results. I couldn't make it tidy, exact, neatly contained. I couldn't understand.

As I travelled further on the Inner journey, this made sense. Theologians, fighting each other to get better and better definitions of 'God'. Never seeing that if God could be neatly parcelled up, labelled, completely understood, then diminishment, by confinement within the scope of the human brain, actually could destroy the whole 'God' concept.

How do we live then, without understanding? On the outside I think it means staying open, receptive, interested, while allowing intuitive leads quietly to comment, 'That doesn't feel right' or 'that's alright for him/her, but not for me' or 'not just now'. Or joyfully, 'Oh *yes*—just what I need' or 'I can maybe explore that'.

And all the while the Ageless Spirit flows within us. All knowledge, all wisdom, all love, waiting patiently for us to allow and foster inner communication, connections, discovery that all life is meant to flow together, love together, create together.

And occasionally there is a truly magical display of this universe law. (And don't we, as humans, try so hard to disbelieve it and make laws of our own, separative laws, that are almost anti-life?) Such an occasion happened to me some years ago, totally unexpected, in an ordinary setting, yet I can still physically feel it, as I remember.

It was market day in the Swaledale village of Reeth—high summer, the cobbles set out with many stalls, the place full of tourists. The locals were out too, buying their fruit, meat and vegetables, meeting friends, standing gossiping. At the far end of the market place Barclays Bank rose up majestically, a flight of three or four steps leading to the impressive front door.

I was standing talking to a friend when out of the bank came a young mother with a tiny girl. She was about two, her head still covered with sparse baby curls. Her mother started to move away, but the little girl stood still, at the top of the steps leading down to the market place. She delighted in the busy scene, loving everything she saw, smiling here and smiling there with abandon. Her smile was absolutely wonderful, lighting her whole small face. To me, her energy was special. 'You are so beautiful,' I thought.

I smiled at her, and to my surprise she turned, carefully negotiating the steps, and came to me—quite a little distance. As she came, I crouched down, to be at her level. She put her little bare arms round my bare arm, and rested her head against me. I dropped a kiss on the top of her head. She looked up and smiled, then continued to cuddle, and got another kiss. I do not know how long she would have stayed, but my friend said, 'Shouldn't you go to mummy, love?' She looked round, her mother held out her hand, and she toddled off.

To be given a spontaneous cuddle from a child I had never seen before felt like a huge gift. Later, I learned that her name was Grace. It fitted. Surely she was grace for me that day—no words, no organised meeting, just a deep and instant communication. I can still remember vividly the feel of the small sunburned arms on my arm. Synthesis, connection, magic.

I had not looked for that, no meditation, no deep thoughts, no attempt to be 'good', spiritual, aware. No setting up of that space or meeting. Why such magic communication? Why me?

As the years have gone on, I have found that such happenings, connections, miracles, hold no apparent earth pattern. Somewhere along the line the plug is inserted, the current directed to the Light, and the miracle can shine. I do not need to understand, just say YES, with joy. For me, certainly, it is easier in the countryside, and wild life quickly homes in to a free flowing Spirit. Some places, too, offer magic easily.

But you needn't just wait—you can start actually looking. Most of us go through life with tunnel vision. No, more than that, with a box over our head, and just a wee peephole. A quick glance at whatever is there, then pass on. 'What a glorious sunset, pity we have to go in.' 'Isn't the garden lovely, masses of colour just now. Would you like a cuppa?'

I've found a concept of truly looking, looking inside as well as out, which I call 'true perception'. Start with something simple, take a flower, stay beside it and really *look* at it. See the petals, the colour, the leaves, the shapes, the light and shade. Start to get to know the *out*side of this flower. Then go further; imagine you are travelling *in*side. What is the flower feeling just now? Share the feeling. Is it happy where you have put it? Can it thrive? Hold an imaginary conversation, perhaps apologise for having picked it (mine are always 'rescue' picked flowers), but thank it for coming inside to give you so much pleasure. Now look again at this flower: look with 'true perception', see it as an expression of the Ageless Spirit, feel your Spirit begin to flow with it.

Interesting, as I wrote the last paragraph, the flowers on my inside windowsill gave me a huge unexpected blast of scent. I always think that a flower uses its scent as an expression of its spirit. What a lovely sharing, saying 'Yes' to me in their turn.

I find that flowers and animals respond very quickly to true perception, perhaps more so than humans. They don't seem to have the barriers we put up: conventionality, mistrust, disbelief, and I've been amazed at some of the lovely communication—it has felt like an honour sometimes, a trust, a recognition.

One day, sitting quietly by the river, I watched a pair of young kingfishers fishing—perching on the branch of a tree, then dropping, like stones, into the river, emerging with a silver wriggle in their beaks. Back to the branch, and then all over again. They were on the far bank of the river and greedily I wished they would come closer, we were so much in tune. I was startled when, thought hardly gone, they flew across to my side of the river, passed immediately in front of me, down river, then back, this time flying so closely behind me that my hair blew in the draught. Then back to the fishing.

This happened in my life when I was only just beginning the conscious travel of the inner journey. I couldn't believe it. Was it coincidence? Or had our spirits touched? Today I would have had no doubt.

One thing I have discovered and that is that stillness and inner connections run together. I am, as a personality, a very quick thinking, quick moving, up and down sort of person. But when I visit the inner space, deliberately or not, I find a given stillness that must, I think, give out peace, safety, and acceptance. It is to this that all life responds. It is in this space that we discover again the life-magic, and the miracles.

Some places particularly reflect this. Near me there is a beautiful arboretum, a place of trees, wild flowers, grassy paths, a lake. It is always quiet there, but on some days the magic is profound. On such days all the visitors talk quietly as they wander round and smile as they pass each other. On such a day, as I sit quietly, a pair of dragonflies land on me, one on my green jumper, one on my hand. This one sits quietly as I raise my hand. Wordlessly we communicate. Moving on, I stop to look at a beautiful peacock butterfly, sunning itself on a post. True perception...gently putting my finger against the post, I invite it to join me. Tiny hairlike feet tickle my finger as it climbs aboard, saying hello by flattening its wings on my finger, in exploration. That finger felt special for days.

And what about true perception with other humans? Easier with people you don't know than with people you do? Familiarity with well-known personality traits can very easily distort the glimpse of underlying Spirit. But practice makes perfect. When I was slowly recovering from ME I had little to do but watch people, along with other life forms, and I tried true perception as I watched. It seemed that people responded differently when, secretly, I was 'seeing' them as strong quiet eternal Spirit, rather than as the fussy, impatient, cross, interfering outer casing they habitually presented. And so of course did I. It was fun to go in and perceive the hidden goodness and joy so often cleverly, if unconsciously, disguised.

I remember one day noticing, perceiving, a tramp, a real 'gentleman of the road' walking quietly, steadily along the country road. I was driving, so it was only a fleeting glimpse. His face was weather-beaten and strong; it felt as though the earth was his, and he the earth, a singing Spirit. I was quite overwhelmed, and only on thinking it over afterwards remembered the shabby coat, filthy boots, and polythene bag of belongings. No matter.

So, start 'perceiving' today. Magic is all around (and within) us. Don't try, don't find a method of search, just be ready to allow, to let the Spirit currents flow and merge. Oh yes, and forget age. Sometimes, when I see a tiny new baby, so small, so fragile, so dependent, I am struck with the wonder that this tiny frame already holds the Ageless Spirit. As we get older, as outer frames weaken, as movement or health or companionship seem to be on a diminishing roll, it makes no difference in reality. The Ageless Spirit never diminishes, is never ill, or sad, or defeated. It just flows on and on and on…All we have to do is say YES and travel with it, share its knowledge.

I believe that sometimes old age is the best space in our lives for inner exploration and confirmation. Our outer bodies may force us to learn to enjoy quiet spaces, be still more often. You can choose. Is this imprisonment, confinement, loss, hardship? Or is it a time to talk more with the angels, move in the Life flow, learn more about the person you were born to be? A time to share too, maybe in person, maybe in thought, the wisdom and ongoing learning that continues to be yours as the inner/outer dualities at last begin to merge, the one travelling companionably with the other.

But what if we turn it on its head? Magic produces happenings beyond my understanding, coming perhaps from depth of Spirit. What if my understanding grows? What if I begin to know how to use and direct energies? What if I start to offer myself as channel for the deep and wonderful energies always available in the Universe: love, healing, creativity? Does the magic go?

In some ways, yes. I can read about the miracles performed by the man Jesus and they may now seem neither magic nor miracles. Why? Because, demonstrably, this man had such awareness of the inner/outer life synthesis, such lack of duality fragmentation. So I can understand that it was possible for him to work from his deep inner life base, redirect energies, act consistently in what might be called a way of commonsense based on 'knowledge', true knowledge, inner knowledge. Part of this knowledge, for him, would include what we have to call the 'secret forces of nature'. To the ignorant or unbelieving this was indeed magic, but not to him, and increasingly not to those of us who are learning the inner ways.

I began this chapter just with 'magic'. Though my original definition stands, that is 'beyond understanding' and though, as I have suggested, as understanding grows this concept may change, even lessen, there is more. I believe that true and beautiful white magic filters, energywise, everywhere, through all those human beings who are in touch with soul and Spirit.

To you, who reads this, maybe old, maybe tired, maybe feeling useless, I tell you, quite certainly, that the Ageless Spirit flows in beauty, through and round you as you journey on. Shining white magic—believe it.

And does the Universe not have a soul too? Does it not sometimes channel this great and stirring Energy that is Love and Synthesis and holds a wide open door to the inner country? This, I think, is what I can feel on magic days at the arboretum. Something I do understand, but something far beyond my present capabilities. Yet strengthening me and opening me to whatever synthesis is right for me on that day, at that time. Touching me with the numinous, the other, stirring songs in my soul, making things happen. MAGIC.

2

COMMUNICATION

Moving on from magic, I want to tackle more specifically the theme of communication in old age. There has been such a leap in technology in just one lifetime that for you, me, the older person, the whole notion of communication must change. For example, those of us in our seventies remember the day when a telephone was an innovation. I remember well our first telephone, a strange looking upstanding instrument, with a handle and a trumpet. To make a call you lifted the handle, waited for a pleasant voice miraculously asking for the number and spoke this clearly into the trumpet. In Scarborough, where my father was a dentist and so invested in one of these new instruments, our number was Scarborough 9!

Nowadays it is so different. Anyone, anywhere in the world can be contacted almost instantly. Emails fly backwards and forwards, pictures as well as words. Mobile phones have become more and more sophisticated and in constant use. The media bombard us with information, news, entertainment, additional aerials, in and out, allowing wider and wider scope.

But this is communication through modern technology. Where do we older people fit in? (I am sometimes, turning off some crude and senseless TV programme, tempted to ask where does Ageless Spirit fit in?) And this is interesting. I know of two women in their nineties who, in this deep rural area, own and manage a great set-up of computers, printers, etc. For them, fairly housebound, life is greatly enriched. I am glad.

At the other end of the scale some pensioners refuse to become computer literate. Why? They say, 'I don't want internet, I want to meet people face to face. I don't want to be invaded by Emails, catch a virus, be worried about things going wrong. And anyway, I can't possibly afford the extra bills.' But, of course, many choose a middle way, and choice is the operative word for them.

I spoke to an older friend the other day who said, 'Thank goodness I still have friends who like to write letters. How lovely to have a great wadge of news and thoughts. I can read, re-read, chew over and then write back, ready to look forward to the next one. And I go to the library, pass all the people working feverishly on the computers and come home with a bagful of books. Most of these I read in bed, propped up with pillows, cuddling a hot water bottle, cuppa on the bedside table. I wouldn't want to cuddle a laptop!'

Communication by technology. What else is there, especially for older people? Is this one area of life where age could be seen as limitation? When we are young we have such a wide network of communication: friends, work, colleagues, partners, children. But as we get older contacts in some of these ways diminish. Too many of my close friends ('close' means more than just discussing the price of tea) have moved on. As suggested in the introduction, some have gone to live with close family members, some into sheltered flats or care homes, and some, of course, have gone through the deathgate and words will no longer reach them. (Not sure about that!)

But we don't have to see old age as a continuing period of loss. Yes, some parts of our lives will no longer remain, but if we *choose*, and again this is the operative word, if we *choose*, we can change things, find other methods of communication, maybe other receptors too. Then loss gives way to discovery, things new, creativity, even in some areas greater fulfilment.

What do we actually mean when we say 'communication'? Back to the dictionary, let's find some definitions. The first, very obvious one, is 'to succeed in conveying one's meaning to others'. Yes, that makes good sense. But I fell in love with some of the other definitions: 'to give a share of'; 'to bestow'; 'to have means of passage'. These, to me, move us immediately to deeper, more meaningful ways of communication.

For on the whole we do it so badly, partly because we are fixated on method. There is a fable about, that communication through language is the great human achievement. No other life-form has this skill—we can say it all. Skill, yes, and personally I hugely enjoy playing with words, tidying patterns, making it come right. With words, too, I try to share the nonverbal parts of my life: the feelings, the physical experience and, most of all, the spiritual insights and discoveries. Is my language adequate? Can I truly 'bestow' with words? I think not.

How many times have you made real effort to communicate with clarity? Perhaps with someone temporarily estranged, perhaps because of, to you, the importance of the content to be shared. So you thought about it, made your spiel totally clear, and finally delivered it. But the person who was listening heard something quite different, not what you thought you'd said at all. How? Because, inevitably, on both sides life experience crept in, maybe in very subtle ways, and coloured the words with different shades of meaning. We think, perhaps, that we are being so reasonable, so logical. No good. Why? Because we are overlooking the emotional content that changes the actual ability of the listener to respond as we expect, from our point of view.

Fed up with communication resting mainly on weather, children, food, or the latest political scandal, I started a women's group. Not as a feminist outpost, nor as an emotional support group, but as a means of sharing women's views at depth, on every sort of subject. We took it in turns to introduce our particular choice of subject and it worked. As we gradually built up trust, we were able to become open and vulnerable and have genuine non-aggressive disagreement. At times I found it absolutely fascinating. How *could* you think that was the meaning? Easily.

Interestingly, as the group welded together, in spite of very mixed ages and background, the subject content became deeper. Almost inevitably we ended up discussing the spiritual dimension. I actually began to find more support from sharing of the inner journeying through this group than through the avowedly spiritual nature of the Quaker Meeting to which I belonged. Why? Because we were attempting to share as whole people. Language yes, but also a good deal of expressed feeling and many physical problems and pitfalls. Open and vulnerable, were we not creatively, in communication, exploring a feminine 'means of passing'?

The wordy sciences seem to me somehow to trip over so many boulders in their path. One thinks again of the theologian, desperately trying to dress God in suitable clothes. The fable of the blind men and the elephant comes to mind. For one, an elephant is a tail, for another a trunk, for another a huge warm body. All absolutely right, as per their fragment. But putting it together...how *can* we describe God in words?

I remember years ago, when I had a much loved partner, sitting at breakfast—what a mundane ordinary time of day—tears filling both our eyes as we looked at each other, so great was our depth of feeling. Then, with a wry grin, embarrassed, we both looked away and got on with our meal. No words, but what a lot was said.

What about the language of music too? Many a time, as I sit quietly listening to Bach or Mozart, I find a real peace and belonging and acceptance in the world. This truly is 'bestowed' on me. Or the language change as I put on a CD of light swirling music that invites me to get up and dance, and I often do. One miserable isolated Christmas I purchased a CD that included the track of the lovely hymn 'Be still in the presence of the Lord'. Boys' voices soared, and it was the music that took me in. 'Be still, for the Power of the Lord is moving in this place' became true as the music spoke to my soul. The loneliness and fear disappeared as I happily cried, in awe and reverence.

For some people it may be colour, with its own language. For some the countryside and wordless sharing there with other life forms. There are no rules, it is all about life interrelationship, communication with respect and love, energies crossing and merging, deep junction with the Ageless Spirit.

And we continue to move towards our inner space. Each of us has a different path to follow. It can be such a delight to accompany someone else on his/her path, a new experience, a different 'means of passage' to recognise. Physicists today are talking about 'emergent synthesis', a true coming together of fragments. And excitingly discovering an inbuilt forward-looking adaptability and creativity in all life processes, even of very primitive species. I wonder how many tens or hundreds of years it will be before it can be formally recognised that all life moves towards s/Spirit—and not fragmented spirit at that. The greatest communication? Some of us, many of us, 'know' this already (but alas, only anecdotally).

We haven't yet looked at thought as a means of communication for both inner and outer being. Like speech, or writing, thought again tends to leap toward fragmentation—it must be in words. And very quickly we discover that word-thought is potent. I pray for someone and evidently they receive and benefit from the result. I send a very determined healing thought to a client, and he rings up to thank me. But is it really just the words? There is more. What about the right side of the brain activity? (Remembering that the left side is the binary computer—logical, building concepts in reasonable steps.) The right side is the analogue computer, holistic, illogical and often only giving us hints of the whole, in picture, symbols, intuitive glimpses.

A friend rang in total despairing agony while waiting for a hip replacement. 'I can't bear it. I can't sleep. I can't take any more drugs—tummy is in shreds. *Please* can you help?' It didn't seem like a logical thinking problem. That night I sat down and pictured my friend wrapped snugly in the softest of pink blankets (rose is the colour, for me, of love), settled her in a tiny boat and let this rock gently on a deep blue lake, under an indigo sky. Then stopped 'thinking' of her, even in picture form, so as not to blur the communication.

She phoned me at ten o'clock next morning. 'What did you do? I've just woken up, my first full night's sleep for months.' What had I done? Here is the mystery—I don't really know. From the Ageless Spirit came the picture that she needed. I shared that energy and she slept. But I knew that this time it needed no words.

What we are really doing is approaching the realisation that communication is made through shared energy. This energy may be expressed in words, but may also be expressed through colour, music, feeling, touch, or any one of innumerable conductors of energy. Lately I have discovered a sharing of healing that involves my belief that I can go deep into my inner space, and just take the person in need with me. I don't need to know why or how, just trust and be. Healing takes place, for both of us.

This energy sharing makes sense with animal communication too. Animals seem to 'know' with a sense not necessarily appreciated by us as mere humans. My cat always meets me on my return home, early or late, waiting in the courtyard as I drive in and rolling on her back to have her tummy tickled as I approach. My last cat did this even when I came back from holiday. But he had not been waiting around, only appearing at the crucial time. What communication did they receive? Certainly not consciously sent by me.

Out on a muddy hillside walk, my small Yorkshire Terrier dashes ahead, enjoying the various sounds and smells. But if I begin to feel slightly apprehensive at crossing a very sludgy muddy patch—might I fall?—he is back in a flash and stays very close till danger is past. Further, if birds and animals cannot 'think' in human ways, how come they can answer human thought patterns apparently presented in words? Remember the kingfisher mentioned in an earlier chapter. My thought pattern was simply 'I wish you would come closer', and suddenly there they were, almost brushing my face as they flew past, blowing my hair in the draught as they flew back. Then, job done, back to the fishing. How was I understood? Somehow, somewhere my energy mingled with theirs. Delight.

It doesn't really make sense. Good. For I find so often that non-sense leads eventually to a much deeper understanding, involving the whole of me sharing with the 'other', whatever, whoever, wherever they may be. If I try to calculate, tabulate, I get stuck within the present functional limits of the brain. (Though I hope many new little pathways are cropping up even there.)

Similarly, perhaps, energy can follow thought in a very sharply focused way when a decisive healing communication is needed. Sometimes people who are ill, lonely, bereaved, cannot cope with thinking, with following systems, with behaving in a reasonable way. Too hurt, too lost, too rejected. Talking as such, is no good. And yet, like the animal reception, a short 'command' thought can cut through the darkness in which the person is hiding.

I remember with amusement and slight shame, the occasion when, quite late in the evening, happily soaking in my bath, I realised I had forgotten a client's request. Sarah's life was going through an abysmal patch, husband impatient of her frequent illness, two tiny children making demands she couldn't meet on her own. Living in a haze of exhaustion, she only had to put her head on the pillow to be wide-awake. Nights were a misery of wakeful endurance. '*Please* help me sleep.'

I had meant to put her on the appropriate radionic treatment, perhaps even boost this with a visualisation. And forgotten. Somehow, on a cold winter's night, the thought of returning to the study, getting out the file, etc., seemed totally unattractive. Still soaking, I focused all the thought power I could gather and sternly declared, 'Go to SLEEP.' Briefly, I saw her tucked up in bed and deeply asleep, and then let the thought completely go. Somewhere inside me I knew all was well.

Next night I decided to repeat this, and continued the procedure through the week, giving the command, then seeing a picture of the result. She rang me about another problem and I asked, 'How was the sleeping this week?'

'Oh,' she said, 'it's been fine, but really weird.'

'How?' I asked.

'Well, it would happen quite suddenly, just as if I'd taken a megga sleeping pill. If I wasn't undressed, it was really difficult to get ready for bed.'

Aha—words? Yes, but with a vast accompanying energy—with clear focus.

What about the communication factor in meditation, contemplation, received intuitive knowledge, even dowsing, healing? Here it almost seems I must be standing at a huge entrance gate to a sometimes forgotten inner country saying, 'Let me remember knowledge, let me explore further, let me have gifts for my outer life now.' And I don't think that's quite right—too much like battering on the door, trying, needing 'success'. I think the key may just be made of trust. Oh yes, I need to go and stand by the gate, take my part in the entrance. But there is no need for explanation, request. If I home in, outer life to the land of the Ancient Spirit, then everything is there for me, just waiting, and all I need to do is be there and allow.

One contemplation exercise I have been given, and offer here to you, is to become so quiet that thoughts can flow past almost unnoticed, and then expect inner communication. Just for a minute or two, with no definitive expectation. Sometimes afterwards there is an immediate brain connection, an idea, an expressible thought. Quite often there is not, but something changes. A few days later there may be a 'coincidental' happening—a spiritual clue. Or a relationship shifts, or a fuzzy bit of knowledge is cleared. On some occasions there is no sign that anything has happened at all. But I can now understand, like Edrin (see Chapter Six), that at some unrecognised level there was indeed communication.

It's a bit like going down to the seashore. Sometimes you find a lovely shell or stone to take home. Sometimes you enjoy the waves splashing at your feet. But sometimes you just stand and *feel* the sea, its mobility, its ebb and flow, its changeable moods. You are just there, sharing.

I received valuable lessons about communication when, some years ago now, a client rang in deep distress. Would I help? This lass had a mentally defective brother who lived in sheltered accommodation in the same town as their mother. He visited her frequently, and on this occasion neighbours had heard her screaming and had rushed in to find him beating her unconscious. Her skull was fractured in various places.

Karen was ringing from the hospital. Her mother, Laura, had survived the operation to save her life, but the prognosis was grim. The consultant had told her family that if she came out of coma it was unlikely she would ever be more than a vegetable.

Of course I did what I could to help, but the family was wonderful. For an entire month they never left her on her own. Day and night someone was with her. I felt that this close and loving connection might well be more potent than anything I could offer through radionics and absent healing.

And the needed focus was given to me. I suggested to Karen that as she sat with her mother she should imagine her mother's brain as a complicated road system—highways, tiny lanes, town roads, all normally interconnected. But now she should notice the many 'Road Blocked' signs, and whenever she saw one she should put beside it a 'Diversion' notice and then in her mind picture the road bypassing the blocked bit, making connections further on.

Sounds silly, doesn't it? But it worked. Her mother came out of coma, though in a confused amnesiac state. Karen doggedly continued with the diversions, connecting, connecting, connecting. It took time. And of course, there were many treatments going on. Nevertheless, eighteen months later, the consultant declared himself amazed at her progress.

Laura will never be a hundred per cent well again. She needs care and attention. But she has quality in her life, can enjoy holidays, recognise and play with her grandson, undertake simple household chores. Best of all, maintain a happy disposition. How much of this was due to the persistent communication from a loved and loving daughter? I do not know. How would you measure? But I do believe, method apart, the constant sharing, loving, indeed 'bestowing', one to another, were hugely important factors in the healing equation.

As indeed was the overlap at that time, for me, between inner and outer consciousness. One snippet of insight, *in*-sight, produced the tight picture focus for this particular situation. Inner and outer merged. Always there is limitless information to be released if we will only cross the spiritual border. As with our outer communication systems, we may need to learn techniques. For myself I find that sometimes I just need to be still and wait. At other times I need deliberately to let my energy flow out to meet that of the other person's need, and to accept energy in return. Information and action, inner and outer energies, melding together. Communication.

And, mundane but true, practice makes perfect. As with other techniques, once learned they can be forgotten, the process just 'happens'. I drive my car now without having consciously to decide which gear to choose, when to accelerate, which mark on the windscreen (my instructor's trick) I must line up with the pavement in order to reverse correctly. I just drive.

It is exactly the same as you learn more and more about inner-outer communication, using whatever learning techniques come your way. Gradually it seems there are fewer barriers, less confinement, more acceptance, trust, and sharing. 'Bestowed' and 'bestowing', a lovely creative diversity of 'means of passage.'

It's a bit like turning a key, opening a door, rounding a corner to a wonderful view—the Universe and all the life/Life it contains. Such excitement, such discovery, such creativity! Believe it. It may be sunshine, it may be snow, sometimes it may be fog. It may be easy, it may be difficult—all are phases of the inner journey. But if somehow we can keep listening to the soul-song of our inner belonging, allowing these energies to flow, mingle, strengthen, LOVE, then surely we are becoming who we are meant to be, children of the Ageless Spirit, communicating its note to all who can hear.

And this, of course, is where the Ageless Spirit blesses us at our present life-stage. In older age we have time and space to explore communication within its flow. No barriers. I can touch anyone, anywhere, anytime with the Love that creates me, maintains me, and waits for me to be open to it, choose it, BE it.

Am I flying too high? Is this possible for ordinary me? Oh YES. Not all the time, probably not now in any 'doing' way, rather by the be-ing—quiet, loved, belonging—sometimes consciously empow-ered by going in, with trust, faith and most of all, through grace.

And I wonder if, I think I 'know', that this type of communica-tion—quietly sharing in the world the very Spirit of Life—is of more power, more use, more value than any other method. Really, I suppose, it is not a method but a living. So…forget the wandering feelings of being out of date, being useless, weak and ineffective. With heart and mind connect with the inner Ageless Spirit flowing through you, and COMMUNICATE.

For your comfort, let me tell you that this can so often be easy, pleasant, and re-enforcing. Whoever you are, wherever you are, whatever your outward limitations, you can cut straight through them and in the bestowing, as always, giving you are also given. Be practical, just sit down in your favourite chair, use your own way of relaxing, going in, and for a little while rest in that particular space.

I have a little patio outside my back door, at present almost over-whelmed with abundance of flowering. Two buddleia trees (one in a pot) pull in bees and butterflies. An enormous lavender bush sends me waves of scent. There is colour, life, and a lovely sense of wel-come and belonging as I settle into my comfy padded garden chair. Usually I use a Love-Peace breathing to settle me in. Yesterday I was given a different phrase—'Inner Life'. In and out with my breathing until I did, in one sense, reach 'home', and was ready to begin: give, share, bestow.

Half an hour went by, energy prickling through my hands as they rested on the chair arm, just sending out healing love, the energy flow, to friends, to people I knew were in trouble, to the unknown, and finally a steady stream of energy through me, the Ageless Spirit, to the Universe. The energy must have been palpable. I was startled

and delighted when two beautiful peacock butterflies left the buddleia tree for a while and rested on my shoulder, my knee. Together
we shared and bestowed.

Afterwards I felt cool, clean, soul-washed and as though I had
been away on a visit. Time to come back to the garden, the everyday, the human boundaries. But not alone. Communication.

3

ENERGIES

I suggested earlier that never mind the precise method, communication occurs whenever energies are shared. Would you like to know more about the energy system within which we belong?

This chapter will be a quick flypast of energy systems and progressions. The material may be quite new to you, and interesting, but if you find it rather over-factual and dull, just skip it and move on to the chapter on relationships—for which, of course, shared energies hold the major key.

What I hope to describe for you is a collection of energy ladders: a ladder of awareness levels; a ladder of energies flowing more and more freely through the major energy centres; a ladder of relationship between the centres and personal evolution, and finally a ladder of balance and fulfilment as soul energy emerges in the place of control, with openness—and Ageless Spirit takes over. Joy.

Where do we start? Right at the bottom. What do we mean by energy? (I expect for us older folk the comment is often, 'I don't seem to have as much as I used to.') How does it work? This is not a scientific treatise—I can only show pragmatically what I have found to be true. Dictionary terms don't quite fit (or is it that I don't?) 'Power of doing work', 'vigorous activity', 'forcefulness', 'capacity of a material body, or of radiation, to work'…From the clutch of definitions on radiation I pull out the relevant 'to transmit wirelessly'.

Yes, I know that one, sitting on the seat in the patio sharing healing, talking to angels, wrapping a person in comfort and sleep. No wires, just flowing energies producing palpable results.

Let's abandon the formula and explore first the ways in which, right now, we personally recognise energy. How is it for you when you say 'I'm full of energy today'? Bubbly? Purposeful? Happy? Content? For me, full of energy usually means that I must do something, work out a plan, visit someone, exercise. This is in the physical area of my being. Spend a few minutes just now, seeing how it is for you. And conversely, what about the days when you may say 'I just feel as though all my energy is draining out through my feet', or 'I just need to do nothing', or even 'She/he seems to suck out all my energy'.

Interestingly, do you add a positive or negative to either polarity? Is it 'good' to be highly energised? Is it 'bad' to be almost energyless? Might you perhaps need to look again at your precise definition of these currents? Is there blame to be attached to you, to others, to circumstance? Can you allow yourself to be sometimes high, sometimes low, in a sort of ebb-flow pattern? This latter is often seen by women as a monthly cycle, even when physical symptoms cease.

The cycle may be there, but other circumstances, other energies, may override the expected pattern. Watch yourself for a few weeks and see how the physical energy comes and goes, can be enhanced, can be diminished. By what? Circumstances, health, relationship, environment, even will? Are you limiting yourself by expectation, especially by the cliché 'at my age'? We all have a biological pattern, but I think it need not rule us.

Let's move on to emotional energy. I am not suggesting that we can draw sharp dividing lines between any energy streams but, roughly, just emotional energy. Have you ever thought of emotional expression and receipt on energy terms? Try it now. What about anger? How would you describe the energy flow of anger? It varies, doesn't it? Sometimes it is sharp and cutting, straight to the opponent's throat. Occasionally it is like a septic sore, never gets expressed anywhere so heats and heats and produces self-infection. And fear.

How does energy expressed as fear affect *your* life? Does it move straight through to the physical and make you feel sick or shaken? Remember, there is no clear dividing line. Do you retreat into a migraine, or a tummy upset, or some sort of bodily pain? Or does it send you to the cupboard for biscuit or cake or chocolate until finally you produce the bodily comfort of fat? Obversely, can you spot some degree of positivity through the energy allied to fear?

What about the energy, too—emotional energy, that is—that you carry with you on a good day? Go out with joy and a smile and it seems that everyone you meet has a smile for you too. It is so catching, isn't it? We are up, we are down, but because energy must flow, then those we meet are caught in our slipstream and suffer, or gain, accordingly.

Then mental energy—how much energy do you allow to stimulate 'vigorous activity' or 'the power of doing work' in your brain and intellect? How do you encourage growth, your move towards wholeness, through this energy? Do you read, discuss mentally, explore? Do you follow creative ideas, listen and learn and extend your thought parameters through interconnection with all life? Recognise, for instance, consideration of the lifestyle of a tiny bird, an opening flower, as potential mental stimuli? Do you perhaps seek out a mental form of meditation, stretching your known mental processes, yes, but also stepping out into the reason that is beyond the present known?

Obversely, are you deceiving yourself into thinking that as you sit, couch potato, receptor of fact after fact, technically bestowed, that you are using and developing your mental energy? Or alternatively, swallowing and probably regurgitating enough books to stock a library, without ever really thinking? To read, receive, is just to be a passive receptor. This is part of your brain function; indeed, you are programming a computer. But until you begin to think about the facts, play with them, share them, discuss and sometimes discard, very little mental energy is used. You know this, don't you? Padding your brain with easy reading, in bed at night, just to shut yourself down for sleep. And of course it is not always easy, as older folk, to find others with whom to discuss and share. Keep looking.

When you have had a quiet look at the way you use or are used by the three basic life energies—physical, emotional, mental—sit down and take a while to see how balanced or unbalanced their flow may be, in and through you just now. Is it the emotional energy that continually gets the upper hand? I know that one. Or are you the bookworm type, or still immersed in business negotiations, or a compulsive computer buff? (Which energy is in ascendance there? Superficially it looks like mental energy, but doesn't it have a fairly hefty emotional constituent?) Where is physical energy manifest in your present scheme of things? Do you actually get physical exercise, do you notice what you eat or don't eat, do you sleep well, relax well, care for your bodily needs? Or have you given up, saying 'I can't do that any more'? (OK, do something else, and if *that* isn't possible, take a deep breath and *be* something instead.)

It is unlikely that, unconsidered, the three energy streams will earn even remotely equal consideration. As you look, as impartially and detachedly as you are able at what goes on, you will pick up relationships, energies flowing together. For you will see not only the interbalance, but the interdependence. The way that you think does actually affect your physical well-being. Emotional and physical reactions, as I have already commented, are even more closely linked. We don't realise sometimes that we can change a downward move by starting at the other end, so to speak. If I am sad for some reason, my walk tends to be slower. I may bend forward, even slightly hunch my shoulders as if for protection. If deliberately I stand tall, walk firmly, then it seems that the emotional energy is affected. I begin to feel better for no reason. Interdependence—concerted flow.

But to go back to the question of balance. When you have discovered which of the three energy streams—mental, emotional and physical—is at present the poor relation, then deliberately choose a small gift you can give just now to encourage that flow. Small gifts, perhaps for a week, before reassessment. If your emotional energy is the one that is being ignored, or put safely under the carpet and if your relevant pattern of thought has always been 'Men don't cry' or 'Stop being so emotional, it won't help' or 'Oh, pull yourself together', then turn it round and start again, find a gift.

What would you choose to give your emotional life a treat? An unhealthy cream cake, a long extravagant bath, a ridiculously light 'unworthy' book? Or a visit to a friend who you know will listen to an honest description of how you feel, and without comment or criticism give you a big hug.

At the end of the week recheck the balance. It may be time to move on to different adjustments. Physical deficits or over-attention may be easy to spot and gifts easy to find. A long walk in the country, a sleep, a lovely sexual relationship—you find out for yourself. Dealing with attitudes, with the way that you think may be more difficult. Maybe your endlessly thinking mental energy needs to be temporarily redirected to simple concrete activity, or diverted by a night at the pub? Or...? Whether by treat or diversion, begin to bring the three into balance, to a concerted powerful creative personality flow.

Does all this seem very frivolous? Not really, for how can I proceed even remotely towards wholeness if I am totally lopsided in the basic survival energies of life? And, of course, as is always the case with human beings in motion, there will necessarily be an ebb and flow—sometimes one energy, sometimes another needing to take precedence. Fine, just as long as one energy is not always the boss, another the downtrodden misery.

Modern physicists tell us we are all 'just energy'. We have already discussed this, but it is still hard to believe as I sit at my very solid table with artefacts all around me. But what a difference to my life attitude if I can begin to believe it! Energy is always on the move, apart from temporarily anchored force fields, and it becomes increasingly evident that my flow affects yours, yours mine as we mingle together. Distance, perhaps time, seems to have little reality. If I think of someone with purpose and focus, they receive that thought and something changes. As I write this book, energy is put into it which you will receive as you read it. You may be next door, you may be a thousand miles away. No matter.

Have you never woken up in the morning with a huge feeling of apprehension or depression? Nothing in your personal life to account for it, but it is there. Then, later in the day, you hear on the radio of a disaster affecting many people early that morning. Isn't it possible that the shock waves, the fear and despair, in travelling across country, were picked up by you, in your vulnerable pre-waking state? I think so.

I remember, some years ago, when living in Swaledale, I had to take my niece to Darlington to catch her train home. The last few miles were on motorway, and it was an easy and pleasant drive. But on this Sunday, as we got near Richmond my stomach started to turn over with a sick feeling of apprehension. Had there been any choice I would have turned back, but it was essential that the lass caught the train, ready for work on Monday. Carefully, I drove on. There was nothing to account for this strange feeling of apprehension until we came to the junction with the motorway. There were the ambulances, the breakdown wagon, just leaving. All cleared up now, little sign of the major accident which had happened, and hit my solar plexus with the engendered fear, just as I got to the Richmond turn off half an hour before.

How much then, we affect each other's lives—all life, in fact. I was fascinated recently to read of physicists' experiments, facilitated now through modern computers, able to work with a vast number of variables, therefore to obtain precise unimaginable results. We are told, for example, that a butterfly flapping its wings in Texas actually alters the course of a hurricane over Haiti, a week later. A few millimetres to the right or left, and the hurricane would have followed a different route.

That result is of measurable physical energy, but what about the energy of thought? What, or who are your small butterfly thoughts affecting, somewhere, anywhere, on the planet? I perhaps can take personal responsibility for my physical actions. I can even start to show care in my emotional outpourings. Have I even begun to take responsibility for good in relation to my thinking? Have you?

We have been considering energy from a purely personal point of view. Right, I must start from where I find myself in life now. But let's move on and explore the more complex esoteric view of energy. I have been dwelling on the three basic 'stay alive' energy streams, but these all merge into a wider deeper schema of awareness. Even this is in flux, for as more and more people pray, meditate, contemplate, open up to the beyond concrete knowing, then the ceiling of awareness lifts and more discoveries are charted. These are not for this book—let's stay simple for now.

And are you wondering what all this has to do with our Ageless Spirit? Ah, this relationship also rests on energies, as we shall presently discover. We are going to scan fairly briefly two energy systems: the seven planes of humanity, and then the subtle anatomy of each living man and woman. The seven planes denote a sort of ladder pattern of evolution toward wholeness, toward spiritual reality, toward the close inner/outer flow of Ageless Spirit within and without us. Life as one-ness.

Start at the bottom of the ladder. Here is the physical energy, keeping us alive on the planet—the actual energy patterning that gives dynamism to our physical expression, called etheric energy. For the experienced dowser it is simple to demonstrate this energy, a spinning pendulum following the familiar line of the physical body.

Next comes the emotional energy, which a clairvoyant sees and describes as areas of colour, clear or dull, colourful or dingy, according to the mood of the particular person. And of course, there is continual fluctuation as emotion changes, aspiration rises and falls.

Then we move on to the mental energy. Again there is colour, and also actual thoughts so creative that they can be seen as separate forms called thoughtforms. We need to look more closely at this mental stage of awareness. For, when balanced, parts of our mental energy become a bridge to the beyond, to the place beyond logic, to a higher comprehensive reason, a Life-reality.

Initially we find that mental energy in the average human is expressed in three ways. First, the mundane everyday thoughts that occupy a lot of our life. 'What shall we have for tea?' 'What time does the train go?' 'Should I go out tonight?' Nothing very deep or important, just fleeting energetic necessities in order to function basically but adequately. Secondly, we carry round with us the energy that expresses our opinion of ourselves. Because most people never consider the impact one person's energy has on another, these beliefs my be considered private. Not so, take a clear example: a young girl goes to a party about which she feels very uneasy. Her thoughts about herself say, 'I don't really fit in at this kind of gathering. I never know what to say. I can't make clever conversation. No-one will want to bother with me.' All this miserable energy gathers about her, and what happens? Unknowingly, it is 'read' by others at the party, she huddles miserably in a corner, and no-one does bother with her.

What about the person who seems to be utterly unapproachable? Tentative remarks are brushed off—almost one feels an intruder. What is the hovering mental energy here? Could it be 'I don't feel safe relating to you (or anyone)'—'keep out'? The message is clear, understood and acted upon without any need for verbal expression. So what about you? What are your self-thoughts? (Watch out for the sneaky little 'old age' assumptions!) If you can feel that you are of worth, with something to give to life, then that is the energy that surrounds you, and impact brings positive results. Try it

But what if that is not at present your self-image? The thing to remember is that because energy is usually on the move, no negative aspect need remain. Act 'as if' you were feeling positive and find that the truism 'energy follows thought' really is practically demonstrable. Of course we have an ebb and flow. Sometimes we are sad, tired, lonely, feel old, insignificant, forgotten. But equally we can change almost in an instant, recharged in a multitude of ways—a phone call, a letter, or just a turn of our personal energy tide. If we *choose* the other polarity, negate these changes, hang onto our misery, then we may anchor ouselves into a negative force field that takes some shifting. We all know folk who get stuck in this mode, drawing to themselves the ghastly compensation seen outwardly as 'Oh, she enjoys her troubles'.

So, the first two mental energy streams can be fleeting, easily changed, sometimes just seeming to blow in briefly on the way past. The third is rather different. This time we use energy in a determined and clearly defined pattern. We make thoughtforms. These have an independent life in that we make them, focus them, and send them off to work for us. Once despatched we have to stop thinking about them, set them free to reach their destination, and trust their adequacy in performance. The thoughtform may be made in words, in pictures, even in sounds and scents, so long as it is clear, uncluttered, and is given a clearly focused destination. We have already had the example, in a previous chapter, of the friend who was wiped out by the immediate need to sleep, on receipt of a thoughtform that was precise and clear and positively blasted toward her!

It is perhaps as well that we do not usually have enough concentration or focus in our thought activities to send effective thoughtforms. I believe that in any energy redirection of this sort there must be a boomerang element. What you send out comes back. Not necessarily at the same time or in the same form. So it behoves you to take care in what you send and be sure of your motive.

Does it sound rather prosaic, an easy-to-climb ladder of awareness? We are climbing the first three steps—physical, emotional, mental—what next? I have not found it like that. Sometimes just integrating these basic energies, as we discussed earlier, is too difficult. My health gives way, so I am physically focused for days, weeks or longer. An emotional trauma comes my way, and I sink. Thoughts run dementedly round and round. Familiar, isn't it?

So really there is no ladder, just a suggested pattern. We have a need, as humans, for patterning. I love the fairly recent scientific discovery, mentioned earlier, that each tiny bit of us, cells, nerves, tissues, is patterned for creative growth and development. But, like astrological patterns, the ladder pattern may be seen as a guidline, not an imprisoning stricture. Definitely I do not always follow the prescribed pattern. Do you? I am up, I am down, and at best, looking back can see that I have travelled. This is awareness on the move.

The best tool I have discovered for moving on, for encouraging growth and awareness, is simply openness. It is absolutely OK not to know, be certain. To wander in the area of maybe, does it work, is this part of my path? And, my goodness, sometimes there seem to be so many diversions or 'road blocked' signs, or just 'no way for you right now'. The older I get, the more I can accept the 'water over the tops of my wellie' feeling, and once dried out, look at why I had to jump in the pool anyway!

Mental energy, in awareness terms, is also sometimes subdivided into lower and higher sections (patterns again). I use the lower mental energy when I think about the concrete areas of life, about practicalities. I plan my shopping, allocate finances, think about building a house, making a baby. All toward practical results that are necessary for survival on the planet. Using the higher mental energy I move into the abstract, formulate and adapt ideas, appreciate depth in music, poetry, science, beyond the presented facts.

Earlier I talked about a bridge. For at this level we begin to be touched by still higher energies—the intuitional, the spiritual—often fleetingly, but sometimes with life-changing conviction. It is as though the lower self, anchored in the physical, contacts the higher self, and recognises the pull of the soul.

For the soul, to me, is some sort of energy, which confirms to me that I am more than a physical presentation—that what I see, hear, feel, is only an edge of some huge entirety, quite beyond my imagination but of which, indubitably, I am part. It is as if, when I am born, I bring with me one tiny part of soul energy which, in relation to the big oversoul, can keep me travelling in the right direction, if only I will listen, to a sort of Ageless Spirit song. And bearing in mind that all life is programmed for creative growth and development, then perhaps this minute anchored soul pattern is also learning. And do its discoveries flow back to a bigger energy, and bigger, and bigger, and so evolution continues…? Could some of my difficult life lessons, well learned, be tiny constructive gifts to soul and spirit and beyond? I would like to think so. Certainly it seems that it is the higher mental energy that contacts the soul, opens to intuitive information and perhaps, over the plodding years, allows clear glimpses of Spirit?

I suggested seven planes in the evolutionary ladder: the first three, etheric, emotional and mental lead to soul contact. The second three, intuitional, spiritual and monadic, lead to a higher Spirit energised level. At the summit of the sevenfold peak is Divine Energy—this and monadic energy are lives away for most of us. Though, if we begin to understand life as a holograph, perhaps not so far as we think; rather, a negation through blindness.

This then is a personal view of the seven planes, the seven levels of awareness. I am increasingly aware of two factors, first that up-and-downness or in-and-outness is natural, without blame, and part of the life I have chosen to live this time, in energy terms. Second, that somewhere within me there is a deep holding energy, the dwelling, so to speak of the Ageless Spirit. Sometimes from there come angels, sometimes just ordinary people, sometimes the numinous. It is my travelling base, the Energy of Reality.

The doorway to this space, for me, is meditation, though meditation is a concept with many interpretations. Oh yes, it is good to sit down and give time to enter the room beyond the door, but sometimes it also seems that the door is open and I can wander in, even dash in occasionally, within an ordinary life occurrence. The main thing is to keep the door well oiled and in use; the inner holding is always there for me. And for you, believe it.

Does it all sound rather vague and idealistic? How does this Ageless Spirit Energy actually flow through and affect me in the everyday process of living the inner and outer life as an ordinary human

being? Another ladder or pattern, the subtle anatomy. We are all
aware of our physical anatomy—bones, nerves, muscles, tissue. But
the etheric energy, energising this outward appearance, has a different, subtle anatomy. Imagine a lovely web of light around and
through you (and isn't just that an energising thought?). It's like an
intricate flowing network with many junctions and crossovers. We
call the main junctions *chakras*, or energy centres, spinning wheels
of energy. As awareness develops in humanity more and more of
these centres are being uncovered. Here we are only looking at the
main seven whirls of energy, running from base of spine to crown of
head.

The centres act as receptors and distributors of the cosmic energies, at first perhaps through only a partly opened state. Imagine
them, symbolically, as fat flowerbuds waiting to open. As we climb
the awareness ladder, more of the centres open, to receive and transmit freely. But, you may ask, from flowing through the energy centres, how does the cosmic energy actually activate the physical body?
It flows through the glandular system. For example, heart centre
energy is directed to the physical heart, circulation, blood, vagus
nerve. Throat centre energy flows through the thyroid gland to control bronchial and vocal apparatus, etc.

The detail is not so important as the realisation that it is the
energy that flows through the centres that holds the body together
and makes it a coherent and actively energised whole. And it is the
soul energy, striving to get through as controller and conditioner of
life that needs the 'open flower' fully receptive to its influence.
Then, in its turn, the centre can transmit, share this energy through
the appropriate gland, for the physical, emotional and mental well-
being of the individual human being. As awareness increases, as the

centre flowers open, glimpses of soul light appear, and higher energies begin to take over. The three base energies begin to integrate and balance and from that integration can develop a soul-personality relationship, and soul influence increases

And now a brief glimpse of the final 'ladder', describing the work of each centre's energy in our human life. The base centre, at base of spine, encourages our physical will-to-be. The sacral centre, through the gonads involved with sexuality and procreation, produces concrete creativity. The solar plexus, at tummy level, is to do with self-awareness—*me*, my needs, my boundaries, my self-assertion. Do you recognise the feeling of being kicked in the gut when this self-identity is threatened?

These three are the lower 'below the diaphragm' centres. As awareness increases, gradually, their energies begin to join with the matching higher 'above diaphragm' centres. Solar plexus 'love for me' begins to blend with heart centre 'love for everyone'. Sacral centre's concrete creativity energy comes into use as precipitation for some of the throat higher creativity centre's ideas and beliefs. And finally, with a lot of soul help, there can be the junction of the physical-will-to-be with the spiritual-will-to-be, energies flowing respectively through base and head centres.

And what has this account given you, I wonder? I hope a realisation that we are made to grow, stretch up, receive Spirit. More than that, that we do this not by trying and worrying, feeling sometimes inadequate, sometimes failures, but just by being open and allowing, and keeping growing. Somewhere within us and without us and through us the Ageless Spirit IS, and it is as if this IS-ness provides a place we glimpse as we travel on. Long before we can reach our destination there are times when we feel welcomed, or awed, or deeply joyful. For me, I think it has been these glimpses that have kept me plodding on. And the sharing with other travellers always adds to my persistence. This is why this book appears, my turn to share.

What is the energy of this inner place, resource, harbour? For me, it is simply that of soul and Spirit around and through me. I believe it is always there, blessing us, changing us, helping us grow if we so choose. And I have found that while around me it can attract dragonflies and butterflies and small remembering children; it can allow communication with kingfishers and produce an extraordinary blue light to further healing for a tiny half dead rescued mouse (see Chapter Eight)—all experiences of a demonstrated respect for *all* life, and of the powerful non-elective Love of the Ageless Spirit. They demonstrate, too, the life-synthesis, which appears to me to be the unwritten purpose of the planet. Just an interflowing Life Energy. Unity in Love.

4

RELATIONSHIPS

Wouldn't it be wonderful if all our relationships were recognisable expressions of the Life-Energy, unity in LOVE? For life is just relationships, no more. Is that going too far? I think not—what else is there? If you have managed to accept the concept that our human makeup is just energy, then the continual movement, exchange, sometimes clashing of the many energies around us, willy-nilly throws us into endless energetic relationships. Perhaps these are boundless, for it seems, as example, that the energy of thought is timeless and spaceless. I think of you and instantly, however many thousands of miles distant you may be, my thought is there. Relationship.

What about relationships in old age? One thing is quite certain—they will change. Someone said wistfully, the other day, 'I seem to go to a lot more funerals than weddings these days.' I know what she meant. Friends of mine, some very close friends of ten years ago, are no longer around. As we said previously, not necessarily because of death—some to residential homes, some moving away to be with children, some wandering away to Alzheimer land. So what do I do? I change too.

Somehow I have to shift focus, widen my view, open to the unexpected, and be ready for *different* relationships. To lose a partner or close friend means I am no longer a member of a mutual propping up society! No-one now who really understands what I mean, what I feel. No-one with whom I can be blissfully angry or sad, or fearful and yet still be accepted as a loveable worthwhile person. So it may be time to stop searching for that, to learn to rely much more on the inner strength actually present in myself. It doesn't seem fair, does it, that now you are getting a bit more slow and fragile, resources vanish—just when you need them most.

But one of the pitfalls of old age is a real risk of being trapped by fixed ideas from the past. I *need* to be cherished, I *need* to be looked after, I *need* someone to talk to me, listen to me, treat me as a being who merits respect. Of course you do, I do, but not any more from one source—that is not part of the equation. Life is all around you, the Ageless Spirit is just waiting for new connections, a freer flow. And oh goodness, you are not alone. It turned my stomach to hear on the telly of the old woman whose diary had only one entry each day: 'Nobody came'. That is extreme, but go to any downtown 'caf' and see the older people sitting on their own, hands wrapped round a last-all-morning cup of coffee just to share the feeling of company.

So what are *you* going to do? The choice is yours. You can make do with the bit of life you've got left, make the waiting for death as easy as possible, fill time with books and telly, and possibly lots of naps. If that is your choice right now then that is right for you. But you can also make the choice of moving on, learning, loving, sharing the Ageless Spirit flow. And this doesn't necessarily even mean leaving your chair. Try it. Give everyone who passes your window a gift. How can I? Easily. How about a simple blessing? 'I give you love, joy, happiness, laughter!' Or a prayer, or a wish, calling in an angel, or a simple mental handhold as you travel into your own deep place and take them with you. Always energy moving, uniting, bringing the Universe together again.

And if there are no people, what then? Then it is time to explore further. Talk to the plants on your windowsill, love them, appreciate them, give them a reason for living. Catch a glimpse of the sky, or treetops, share the sudden fury of a rainstorm, the bright warmth but sometimes ruthless exposure of the sun. All these relationships…allow yourself to flow free in all the life energy around you. Everything, including you, belongs together, wants to flow together. All you need to do is just jump in and start floating along in the life current.

Does this sound too airy-fairy? I have to admit, a hang-up perhaps, that when I read all these wonderful spiritual books describing how you reach advanced knowledge, what practices you need to follow, what goals to reach, I back off and ask myself, 'Is it real?' Is it too much to say 'You need never be alone when in the spiritual life you have all power…You are choosing your present life, you do not need…'? At one level, YES, but I still wish, coming in tired from shopping, that an ordinary someone would be there to say, 'Shall I get you a cup of tea, love?' Duality remains—a part of the puzzle. I should make it quite clear that I personally do not pretend to have the answers to life, to love, to be-ing. I don't believe there are 'the' answers. As you make your own journey you will find your own solutions. If not, you will look further, and that's what it's all about—not stopping, moving on, joyfully anticipating.

What I have found for myself, in relationship terms, is that, meditating and following a 'stillness, joyful anticipation, trust' basis for my travels, I can sometimes recognise a magnetic pull, a junctioning. As I reach out, in ways practical, physical, emotional, mental, then back to me, possibly in a different manner, new connections appear. Give and receive, receive and give—two sides of the same energy.

Because we are travelling on the inner journey, rediscovering, reconnecting with the Ageless Spirit, life and spirit Source, I am going on now to consider just three main areas of relationship. (But don't let this stop you exploring many, many more.) The first, though most important, is often overlooked—relationship with oneself. The second is relationship with other humans, and indeed all life forms. The third, relationship with the energies of soul and Spirit. Inevitably, all these interrelate; we are only separating for clarity.

So, let's look first at ourselves. 'How do I relate with me?' Perhaps that question can only be answered with another question: 'Who am I?' I believe that everyone is born with a need to fulfil the potential of that particular life. And that the main life task may be just that, to become the person I was born to be. It is horribly likely that a lot of this person has never surfaced. Why not? Because well meaning parents, teachers, partners have all had a go at shaping me into what *they* think is best for me (Or for them?). I remember years ago going to a transpersonal workshop and being led through a visualisation exercise which began by asking us to picture ourselves at the start of an heroic journey, and then give ourselves names. The picture came immediately, but I could not find a name.

Discussing this later at a counselling session, my very wise counsellor suggested, 'I suspect your identity has been totally smothered by your parents' expectations. You do not have a name as yet, because your true identity is not strong enough to be labelled.' They had schooled me, she felt, to be intellectually dominant, but my truly dominant factor was intuition, finally uncovered after nearly a fifty-year wait through 'coincidence' arising in my life, clarified by a skilled intuitive counsellor. Certainly, once I took a deep breath and let myself experience intuition, my life blossomed.

So who am I? A system of flowing and anchored energies, giving and taking in the world, and beyond the world. Patterned for growth and fulfilment, but sometimes fiercely resistant. Needing balance of the three basic energies so that, integrated to a single flow, these can more positively affirm growth potential. As this begins to be realised, and if openness and vulnerability can be accepted, then I can welcome the more subtle soul and spirit energies. Through these I can begin to experience and shape energy patterns that lead me truly to become who I was born to be.

Does it sound very self-seeking, this 'ideal' relationship with myself? Oh yes, for I am still cluttered with other peoples' imprints, particularly those that relate to strict childhood moralities. 'Be good, put other people first,' even the lovely FHB, one family's reminder, when entertaining that 'Family holds back'.

But turn it on its head and see how others benefit if 'myself' comes first. Does this sound crazy? Not so. If I know I am of worth, and if I know that I have gifts to offer that to me speak of true creativity and growth, if I no longer need to defend myself fiercely at all times, then what happens to relationship with others?

Clear about my identity (and probably making many, many mistakes as I explore this) I can not only happily be myself, I can welcome other peoples' real selves as well. 'Why ever does that clever lad waste all that brainpower? Fancy, just working on the land', or 'There's no money in that for her, listening to peoples' problems all day long. Why didn't she go into a job with prospects? She's clever enough.' Can you hear the imprints? Somehow this lad and lass have managed to ignore other peoples' expectations of them, found the place they need to be just now, and will doubtless blossom there until it's time to change. Change, for them, will not hold too many fears, and who knows where they will be in ten years time? Maybe still not in the money, but very much in the life.

If I can persevere in uncovering my true identity, then I believe I will necessarily uncover 'that of God in me' as Quakers say, the seed of love and caring and service. Strangely, the people I can help, and with whom I can share, will come to me as and when there is a need—the magnetic factor again. Perhaps one of my—of your—jobs is to nurture those who are still buried under someone else's imposed patterns, or held down with wickedly high tensile moral strictures. I may well not need to do anything, but just be me, a person who is daring to be open and exploratory, and trustful. It is infectious.

But why is my relationship with myself so important? Simple. If you build a house you don't put the roof on first, you start with the foundations. Possibly you don't even start there, for you have to check that the ground below is solid, has no hidden fissures, is not a thin layer disguising mine shafts. Then you can proceed. If I want to grow, to contact my inner strength, to know more about my spiritual life, I have to start from where I am. The more knowledge I have of my starting point, the stronger the new building. The wider and deeper my relationship with myself, the more I can offer to new growth and development.

It isn't easy. I may find I don't actually much like the person I am right now. I may fall into the trap of 'Oh well, I'm not very talented' or 'I'm the emotional type, nothing I can do about that' or—and this is the common one—'I had such a dreadful childhood, you can't expect me to…' Excuses, excuses, excuses, and now, of course, 'I'm far too old to change'. Alright, stay where you are rather than face up to working on this so important relationship.

I will tell you something. Change *is* possible! It is never too late. Say 'YES' to Life and it will support you in undreamed of ways. Believe it, for it is true.

The first task is just to get to know yourself, hidden below the many imprints. The second is to accept yourself. Oho. I remember with clarity the woman of about sixty who came to see me, completely unable to decide what next. She sat down in the study, looked at me, and with obviously huge bravery announced, 'I'm a lesbian.' No rockets went off. I commented, 'Yes?'—and waited for the next bit. It was a horrific story.

This woman had never had a close relationship with anyone, had not even known herself well enough to uncover her sexual preference. I suspect she didn't want to know. Her job was a civil service one, and in their large office was a young girl of whom she became very fond. She made absolutely no sexual advance but unwisely, and innocently, made her strong affection for the lass too apparent. The girl took fright and reported her. Here began the horror. She was moved from the department and told that no further action would be taken if she promised to see a psychologist. This she did.

For eighteen months this woman suffered under the hands of an ignorant insensitive man. He told her first that she had an illness, but this was curable if they persisted. Second, that it was an evil condition, so she must be glad she had the opportunity to be cured. Pension age rescued her. She moved back north, and finally came to me. She was the first person I had ever worked with to have virtually no self-identity. He had blazed away her natural bent, written off all her skills as worthless because of her 'evil ways' and made her a nothing.

I just looked at her, this poor shadow of a woman, and wondered how long it would take her to rediscover her identity. It took a long time. She came for an hour every week and I was fascinated to hear of the timid sorties she made out into the real world. She soon discovered I really did appreciate and respect her and that her sexual preference was a part of her that was absolutely genuine and acceptable. I saw her potential as a healthy creative person, as I practised true perception.

Gradually she found herself. I was glad to hear that quite quickly she discovered Buddhism. It seemed that her spirit, chained for so long, was leaping out in relationship. And then a strange thing happened, which totally affirmed her growing faith in herself. A man who had known her for many years, rather older than herself, came back into her life and wanted to partner her. She came in to see me and told me, 'I said to him, I couldn't partner any man, that's not right for me—I would need to find a woman. Sexual relationship with you is out of the question. I'm sorry.'

Confidence to say that! I felt like cheering. And it worked out so well. The man was very wealthy and they came to an amicable arrangement. Every two or three months he took her on a wonderful holiday, separate rooms, no suggestion of hanky-panky. He asked her again if, on those terms, she would marry him. It might have been a tempting security, but she refused, saying marriage was obviously not for her, and she felt she would have been denying her own reality.

Her Buddhist faith deepened and her life blossomed. But this had only been possible through the development of a healthy accepting relationship with herself. Not everyone will have such a dramatic almost total restart. But look at your*self*—which bit of you do you insist on denying or keeping secret?

It's not too late, really it isn't. Open the prison doors and let out all those lovely bits of you, never acknowledged because of other peoples' censorship. Escape and flourish. Exciting, isn't it? And if you don't like all you see, you can change. Energy always wants to flow, be courageous—let it.

It's odd, isn't it, that we are so hard on our selves? Someone else's behaviour may make me angry. Usually, I try to sort it out. If that isn't possible I have to walk away and let it go. (Easier if I believe in me and don't need defensiveness). Often I can see a genuine mistake that allows a fairly easy 'forgiveness' both ways. But oh dear, if I behave badly, if I say the wrong thing, I can beat myself up for ages. Why? It doesn't get any easier, does it? We can see now, with terrible clarity, some of the past mistakes in our long lives, recognise them as mistakes, and yet still find it hard to forgive ourselves.

What makes me think I can be perfect? There is no reason for everyone to like me, so why do I feel inferior and put down if I am not regarded, if other people are favoured in my place? Fencing off the Ageless Spirit, it is as if my internalised mother is saying things like, 'You mustn't do that' or 'nice little girls don't fight or argue or be rude' or, worst, 'They won't like you if you don't behave.' You will have your own dialogue and I'm sure, as you read this, some of the comments you have nourished for years are *still* alive, and *kicking*.

So long as they are nourished, these poor internalised children, yours and mine, never get a chance to grow up, remain defensive, hurt, sometimes aggressive in seeking protection. And oh dear, how they manage to pop up, in all the wrong places, in your outwardly adult life.

Sometimes we need help to let these children go. To transform also the inner mother—true part of us?—so that she can be appreciative of our effort, encourage us, and love and forgive us when we inevitably make mistakes.

Quite by chance I found a self-help method which really, for me, can change a difficult situation, let me stand back and watch, and allow me unlimited approval. This is a relationship with another of my inner children. But this is one who will never need to grow up. I call her (a girl in my case, yours might be a boy) my 'special-to-love' child. To find him or her, sit quietly, close your eyes and imagine a pleasant outdoor place: garden, park, country, seaside. Then just ask this child to visit you. Watch the picture—he or she will come.

My special-to-love child remains about three years old. She looks very like me at that age—plump, very short dark hair slipping out of its slide, sticky out teeth within a big grin, an imp of mischief. I love her dearly, just the kind of child I seem to get on with so well, even today.

The first time you meet him or her, ask what she would like to do? A treat? Go on a trip, a walk, a paddle? Climb trees, have a cuddle, whatever. Get to know this child well, a lovely child, like an unexplored part of you. Shut your eyes, go in and meet her often. She is your friend and loves you. Sometimes you may need, in your imagination, to put her to bed, read to her, kiss her goodnight. Sometimes she may be ill. Find out why, and do what it needs to make her better. Often she can explain to you what is wrong with the hurt or difficult other inner children (the afraid or angry or sad ones) and can help you put it right.

Mine is still, some years later, an endless pleasure. If I am feeling down or lonely I think of her, and in she bounces, full of ideas, or suggestions, and is good company. She affirms this bouncing side of me, too often unacknowledged. She will come out with me sometimes and make me buy something slight and silly—a cream bun, or a brightly coloured pencil. She will be there when someone gives me unwanted criticism and just giggles. She can see it is ridiculous, then so can I. She has a quality of exploration and acceptance, no hiding who she is. I expect that on my deathbed she will have grown wings and be coming with me. Special-to-love indeed.

As I learn to relate to myself and find my worth, things change in my life. I begin to uncover and sort out some of the twisted knots of past (and present) emotional energy. I let my physical body have a better time too: more exercise, proper food, more time for relaxation, even more sleep. If I am ill, I ask myself why? Equally important, I find who can help me get well, without personal diminishment. More than that, with shared creativity. I have certainly found, in this lifetime, that illness is often saying 'Stop, look and listen'. If I don't, it isn't very long before there I am, ill again, probably with different symptoms. Don't forget, we are programmed toward growth and creativity. Block these and the system breaks down. (Conventional medicos call this 'stress', or 'virus'.) In getting well again, remember that focused thought is a primary factor in energy direction. In your new self-relationship perhaps you can stand back a bit, and watch what surfaces? Ouch!

Does it all sound a bit too neat and tidy? It is difficult to write factually without a fairly precise pattern, but life is not like that. One step up and two steps down, occasionally a rung gives way and you seem to be at the bottom again. Don't forget, though, the occasional leaps, when the ladder is left far behind and, if only briefly, you are soaring. In practical terms, sometimes my emotional energy behaves beautifully, or so I think, but my body suddenly protests. Sometimes my thoughts have no apparent focus, so I do well in thought-diminished chore jobs. One energy flows free and true, another just about fades out. And just once in a while a small spark of inner focus blazes up and redirects me.

At first this inner flame is so elusive. I feel in tune with *some*thing. My ordinary down-to-earth energies flow happily and life holds purpose. Then *whoops*, it is gone again. I have tuned out, albeit unconsciously. Perhaps we shall understand better as we probe the relationship between ourselves and the energies of soul and Spirit.

Before that, what about our relationship with other life forms, including the human form? Can you see now how relationship with our own selves is so important as we reach out to others? Why do we feel so uncomfortable with some people, even dislike them, for no known reason? Because of incompatible energies, yes, but I suspect that almost always there is the additional reason that one or other of us is in a deficient relationship with him or herself. I think too that there is some truth in the adage that the quality we most dislike in another person is the quality we personally share. The woman who is so obviously, so sickeningly manipulative, for instance—so where in *my* life is the secret manipulation occurring, and is it effective? Do I really want it to be effective? Ah me. The man who is overbearing and dominant, for if not he feels put down and loses his masculinity. Do *I* feel happiest when in control, diminished, if my view is unacceptable? Watch these intensely disliked attributes, for they can be useful mirrors.

The other way to encourage incompatibility is simply through defence mechanisms—lack of self worth yet again. I am told that at times I can appear extremely self-contained, self-sufficient, even haughty. When does this happen? When *in*side I am an emotional jelly and automatically put on defensive cover. The effect? 'Keep off, I don't want to know you.' Is it surprising that energy repels contact at that time and what I feared happens? But I have set it up. I read somewhere that the only safe life position to hold is the vulnerable one. To me that thought takes some unravelling, but I think it may be true. We'll explore it further later.

And as with ourselves, our relationship with others is so very much affected by the energy imprints of our parents, teachers and later, I find, our children. 'This is how you should behave, judge, criticise.' 'This is what you should read, consider, learn.' 'These are the people suitable for your relationships, these are not.' Sometimes, frighteningly, 'This is the only right approach to the spiritual.' It sounds almost cruel, this so-clear domination. Too often it is much more subtle. Have you ever noticed, really looked, to see how many of your attitudes and beliefs are truly self-engendered? Then take it forward, see what has happened between you and your children. See how your standards and beliefs have infiltrated your relations with your young, subtly maybe, but nevertheless with the hidden message 'This way is the right way'. Did you ever see the need to make it clear that this is today, tomorrow may be different? And that exploration and search are essential factors in the creative development of the 'whole' human being?

This infiltration, I have found, very much affects our relationship with all life forms. I feel deprived without animals and plants about me. Why? In part, I am sure, because my family has always had animals. Plants too. Our mid-town house had a minute garden, but my father made it blaze with colour, wallflowers in the Spring, bedding plants later. The one long thin bed in the back yard hosted loganberries, a fruitful treat in late summer. So much for so little.

I tend to feel that children who are not allowed to have animals miss out on very basic life lessons. If you have a hamster, then you have to keep its cage clean, see that it is fed and watered, and play with it. Even if you don't want to today, its needs are always waiting and must be met. Good practice for later life chores, but also a steady affirmation that all life needs love and care if it is to flourish. Relationship setting—often for life.

A couple of years ago I moved to a flat with a garden—such a sad garden. Straight narrow beds against two walls, little squares cut from the turf on another, each containing a stick-like bush, failing to thrive though planted five or six years before. Few flowers and, to me, a general plea of 'Oh, HELP'. I moved in the February, not the best time to transport plants, but never mind. I *need* life around me, so splashed out on a contract gardener to see what we could rescue. We tossed a clothesline around to make curvy shapes and dug away deep beds right round the garden. I spent a whole day planting slips from the last garden and friends who visited brought more. Every cutting flourished, and by the time the real summer had come clematis and honeysuckle were scrambling up the walls, perennials were bursting with colour, a much loved wild rose was almost shouting with delight.

It was a north-facing garden, subject to a strong cross wind, so why did it decide to flourish? I know why. I just loved it! Every day I went and encouraged the weaker plants, added feed, cut back and, most important, said, 'Thank you.' We needed each other—relationship.

I honestly believe that love-and-care is the best fertiliser a plant can have, that *any* life can have. Love and care, qualities of our inner harbour, soul and Ageless Spirit.

How do I approach this relationship? How do I develop it, how do the mutual energies blend? What happens in my outer life when the energies from my inner life flow free? I think it goes back to my definition of this life task, becoming who I am born to be—by being in my *now*, allowing life to flow through me, by listening to the kind of tiny inner bleep that lets me home in to the signals always broadcast from the inner land, the Ageless Spirit. That is the approach.

As I begin to learn the inner language, trust my intuition as interpreter, listen to the inner tune sounding faintly everywhere I go, harmonious in a wonderful life chorus, as I make space *out*side just to breathe and go *in*side, then this precious relationship builds. And though so often, as older folk, we just plod on, perhaps outwardly overburdened, tired of grieving, I can tell you with certainty that through the deepening inner-outer fusion there flows in serenity, creativity and wisdom. It feels like a sort of slotting into place, a meaning as yet perhaps undefined, purpose, Light in the Universe.

How do I practise this soul/Spirit relationship? Why, with everything around me. If I know even a very little about the very centre of life, then I can recognise it wherever I look—my small warm waggy dog greeting me ecstatically in the morning when I get up, my large haughty cat stalking in and yowling, 'Breakfast's late, breakfast's late, hurry up!' So different, yet so the same. You may be surprised; if you *expect* to find the inner showing through the outer, then you will, in all life. *Each life form in its own way seeks the Life connection, with love.*

The same small dog frequently shames me, for she genuinely believes that everyone is lovely and shows it. Once off the lead, as we walk by the river, she rushes up to every other walker, greets them, then lies down and rolls over to have her tummy tickled. One or two people look down at her with disdain, but most crouch down and melt, as they say, 'Isn't she lovely?' They enjoy the cuddle and go on their way, smiling. Simple expectation of giving love and getting love. I can't always manage that.

The flowering plants on my windowsill are thanked every morning as they welcome me, often with scent, and over the mantelpiece I have a picture of the bluebell wood in the arboretum that gives me so much strength. My ashes are going to be scattered there and while I was walking there the other day I thought, 'If there were nothing else, but because of me more bluebells were going to grow there, that might be enough.' It is a joy now, and it will be a continuing joy then, to add to the inner music coming from that place.

But I'm saying that I need to practise this inner relationship with everything around me. What about with humans, so much more difficult? Why are we, as humans, so good at camouflage? Why are we so busy that we hide the inner flame under a positive blanket of outer activity? Running away? Even now?

I recently picked up a wonderful book *The Tao of Pooh*. Our family delighted in Winnie the Pooh, and here he becomes—yes, the bear of very little brain, but also the bear seen as incredibly wise by just be-ing in the *now* of life. Rabbit is so busy he is missing it. Owl so clever he couldn't reach it. Eeyore occupied with grumbling about it. But Pooh was the bear who followed the Pooh Way, working with the natural order of things, operating on the principle of minimum effort, being 'sensitive to Circumstance', and leaving the mind remarkably empty so that it can be clear and responsive to spiritual energy. He didn't of course use that kind of language. He just *was*.

This tells us so much about the relationship to hold with soul, forgotten inner country, Ageless Spirit. We need that wisdom beyond cleverness, reason beyond logic, space that allows clarity, contentment that comes from just being, as nearly as we can, the person we are meant to be. This wherever we are, whoever we are, in company with you and you and you as you too learn the nothing path to everything and be it well!

This is one way, perhaps your way, perhaps mine, fostering this deepest relationship as we travel. I recognise great truth in it. But I can only see my present bunkered view of truth, you yours, and you may, as I have done, need to diversify and explore different paths. Some are wordier, some see themselves as scientific exploration, some are embraced by organised religious practices. In any continuing relationship there must be change. Though I suspect, as wisdom increases and anxious seeking lets go into a quieter acceptance, then the spiritual integrity found by just being in the now guards against too many diversions.

Is the now changing, or me within the now, and is this part of the ongoing inner-outer relationship? As the focus of my energy changes, inevitably the energy of my various relationships alters. Life itself seems to change as I begin to know myself, to relate to the now of my present environment, and to hear more clearly and consistently the song of the Ageless Spirit broadcast, if I listen carefully, through everyone I meet.

And it is love that carries the notes, your love, my love, their love, for here is the continuing steadfast relationship. And oh yes, together we listen to the song of the Ageless Spirit wherever, however demonstrated. But also, wherever we go, however we be, can you see that it is important that we too keep up the singing?

5

ANGELS

And then there are angels. Do you believe in angels? Last year, researching for another book, I put the query to almost every person I met. And not once did I get a 'No'. A lot of 'I don't know', sometimes 'I don't know, but...' And a positive flow of angel stories.

Why am I including angels here? Because this is another huge area of relationship available to us as older people. We have looked at 'true perception', seeing glimpses of the inside of a person. We have looked at the way all life forms accept relationship when offered. We have seen the often difficult relationship with ourselves. Now it is time to go further, to consider relationship with energies we can't usually see in a defined form—angels.

I discovered three main areas of belief in angels. First, the defined system of angels and archangels, a sort of angel hierarchy, ranging from the lowest manifestations, the elementals, up through devas, to the many categories of angels and archangels. For many people these last angels are seen, or imagined as magnificent heavenly beings on a stage of awareness far greater than our own, unapproachable except through prayer and supplication. The feelings appropriate in such a relationship would be similar to that with human royalty—a little distant and with respect and humbleness.

The second area of belief is focused on accounts or experiences of angels coming in times of great need, and producing miracles of help and fortitude. Some of these stories are, so to speak, acute. There is the lovely story of the three-year-old who was trapped under an automatic garage door. His mother found him, deeply unconscious, lifted the door and got him to hospital. For two days he lay unconscious; then, to everyone's amazement, his recovery was complete, injuries negligible. But more amazing was the story he told his parents some time after his return home. He said he had hurt so much, until the 'birdies' came and helped him. They took him far, far away to a lovely place where there were so many beautiful 'birdies'. He wanted to stay with them, but he said a lovely Light cuddled him and said, 'I love you, but you must go back.'

Then this small boy, speaking in more grown up language than his usual childish chatter, went on to explain further. He said birdies were always with us, but 'We don't see them because we look with our eyes. We don't hear them, because we listen with our ears. But they are always here, you can only see them in here.' And the little boy put his hand over his heart. With limited vocabulary, no formal concept of death and spirits, 'birdies' were his description of beings that came from beyond, and because they were up in the air were like birds, that also fly.

But often these experiences are much more down to earth. People see angels in human form—a man suddenly appearing to give directions in a strange city, then just vanishing. There is a lovely story from an elderly lady who was setting out on a long journey south, to organise her mother's 100th birthday party. She was anxious about the journey and dreading making the various arrangements. Then a young man boarded the train and sat in the adjoining seat. She described him as beautiful, slight, high forehead, carefully combed long straight hair caught in a ponytail. He said he was returning from a visit to his parents, who missed him greatly. He worked as a gardener, spending one day a week out, training at the nearby horticultural college.

For most of the long journey they talked, until finally he moved to a double seat, stretched out and fell asleep. So why was he an angel? Because, she said, he was sent to give her courage. Everything went much better than anticipated, and long afterwards she used to conjure him up in her mind's eye to give her comfort and reassurance. She later said that her idea of an angel was 'someone who is sent by God on a mission of mercy, and who is given heavenly attributes for that occasion'. She knows that the lad is probably busy digging gardens again, but to her he remains 'my angel'.

The third area of belief is in what you might call 'everyday angels'. And the more you learn about angels, the more you begin to set up angel relationships, and the more you can call on them every day, in ordinary life. I have a wonderful angel of my house, not seen in angel form but as a delicate spiral of light, circling the base of the house then going up and up into the sky. As I write I have a candle burning for my angel of writing. Sometimes, when out with the dog high in the dales, I see the sunlight shimmering on the river, the lambs in the fields, the first shy shine of violets by the path, feel at the same time the awesome strength of the fells and sky and sun, and I just stand and thank the Angel of this Dale for looking after it so well.

There is no limit to these everyday angels. They are there, in whatever form you choose to see or know them, waiting to beam in with love, and help.

My own focus of belief has somewhat changed. My personal experiences and the many stories I have heard make me think that angels are really the expression of one beautiful area of awareness beyond our own. Someone suggested they are 'stepping stones to God', another 'footprints of the soul', another 'wires of the Universe'. All these make sense, in that they are attempts to describe powerful energies that cannot usually be seen, as the small boy explained, 'with our eyes'.

But we are given imagination as an *inner* sense of sight and within our human boundaries find symbolic ways of recognising higher energies and, if we so choose, relating to them. And there is no right and wrong in this. Angel energy is beyond the duality in which we live. I have, for example, personal knowledge of my angel of strength. I see him as a large powerful African male standing tall, silent, and watchful. When I need support, say for a difficult confrontation, he is there, standing behind me. On more than one occasion I have felt a firm hand on my shoulder. Once, I remember, he gently took me by the shoulders and turned me round—to face the situation which frightened me. But your angel of strength may look quite different, be a different nationality, different sex, a symbol of strength for *you*, seen with *your* inner sight.

And what if you are the sort of person who finds visualisation difficult? Then for you other senses will be stirred as the angel energy is called for. You may always hear a quiet sound, maybe music, maybe throbbing rhythm, or perhaps a lovely singing silence. Some people find a scent drifts past. There are no rules. All I am saying is that angel energy is real, always present, and only needs for you to ask, for it to come into action for you. You may be asking the Archangel Michael to protect and strengthen you, or Gabriel for clarification and purity, or Rafael for healing. This is approaching the somewhat awesome hierarchy, but the chatter of the little angels of comfort, creativity, tenderness, persuasion, works from the same powerful angelic energy, just differently presented, according to your need.

My guiding angel, only recently reorganised as such, has turned up, as an old woman, in many a visualisation exercise over the years. Just thinking of her makes me smile. Her name, I am told, is Martha, and she is a very ancient looking little woman, sparse greying hair scraped into a tiny bun on the top of her head. She always wears a ghastly hand-knitted cardigan, which washed and better washed, hangs shapelessly almost down to her knees. Tiny she may be, but her directives are short, sharp, and to the point. Recently I joined a correspondence course about angels and as it was in its first year we were asked to give feedback. So…Find your guiding angel and record his/her remarks to you. Beautiful comments poured in. 'You are doing so well',' We love your persistence', etc., etc. What did I get? 'Belt up, shut up, and get moving.' She was absolutely right—stop theorising and off-putting, get on with it. And I did.

You will know the saying, 'When the student is ready, the teacher appears.' The same may be true, I feel, about angel contact (Is it your time now?). Certainly, for the first two beliefs outlined, it seems that times of great vulnerability, sorrow, pain, grief (and occasionally great joy) leave us open to the angel energy. Theories, doubts, cynicism just vanish—the angel is there. Such was my first awe-inspiring contact, an experience indelibly printed in my mind.

My daughter was in hospital about eighty miles away with her new baby, Luke. As I came in from an evening meeting the phone was ringing. 'Did you know the baby was very ill?' Another call, another friend, the same news. Quickly, I rang the hospital. Sister brought Mary to the phone. In tears she told me that the baby had collapsed, was in intensive care, and if he lived through the next 24 hours...Shall I come? Next morning was too long, so after a flurry of arrangements, dog, cat, petrol, I set off across the moors. I didn't realise at the time, but angels were also driving. My beat-up mini must have travelled at over 80 m.p.h., well beyond its limits.

It was a perfect night, very dark and still, the sky spangled with stars. Strangely content, I found myself singing the Quaker hymn 'Dear Lord and Father of Mankind'. And then it all began. The sky to the right of me was completely filled with an enormous angel. Brilliant autumn colours, huge wings outstretched, he was an awesome sight. I never saw his face, as my eyes were pulled downwards. His feet were a short distance above the ground and below him, on the ground, lay a tiny baby. I knew then that the angel had come to take Luke home. When I reached the hospital I found that he had indeed died just at that time.

The funeral was some time later, delayed for the sad post-mortem discovery of a healthy baby succumbing to a hospital infection. It was quite a big event, many friends came to say goodbye and there were toddlers and babies in the church. I had dreaded facing the pain of the day. How could you sing in celebration of this wee life, choked up with tears? But it wasn't like that—there were angels there.

The first hymn was for Luke: 'All things bright and beautiful.' Courageously I opened my mouth to sing and, startlingly, beautiful bell-like sounds echoed through the church. After the service the other granny turned to me and said, 'It must be wonderful to have a voice like yours.' I just said 'Thank you', feeling it too difficult to explain, 'Well it wasn't really me.'

A few months later, in hospital for a major operation, back came Luke's angel. It was the day of the op and after watching the others in the ward eat breakfast I finally got back into bed for the pre-med…and became aware of this vast angel, lying the full length of the 32 bedded ward, head at my end, feet at the door. The effect on the ward was remarkable; a peaceful silence filled the room, people were whispering to each other, and perhaps only I knew why. He was gone when I came back from theatre, but much of the energy remained and I recovered in double quick time.

And that was the end, it seemed, of my angel experience. I remembered it very clearly, but there was no apparent angel relationship set up, no real life change for me. I think I didn't know then about everyday angels. Until, twenty years later, along came notice of the correspondence course 'Working with Angels'. My main reason for joining was that, as a trial run, it was cheap. And I didn't have to travel to it. But oho, 'when the student is ready…'

Conscientiously I followed the exercises, gave the required feedback, and once again moved back into the angel world. I met my guiding angel, my angel of strength, and a wonderful, wonderful angel of wisdom, who I could visit at any time for information. A scatter of others relating to my everyday life, at work, at play, in relationship.

And then, just a few weeks ago, re-connection with Luke's angel. My dearly loved elder brother, 92, was in hospital slowly, slowly dying, mainly of old age. Any quality of life was vanishing; it was time to go, but somehow he couldn't let it happen. Lying in bed one night, thinking about him, I suddenly remembered the night when I watched Luke's angel come to take him home. And I knew that that was the answer. Going into my own quiet space, I talked to this angel, remembering his visit for Luke, and asked him, quite simply, please would he come now and take my brother home? It was very calm and peaceful and just before I went to sleep I sent my mind across to the hospital where my brother lay and told him, 'You will have a beautiful angel come to you tonight, to take you home. Go with him, have a happy journey.'

It was no surprise to have my sister-in-law ring the next morning to tell me that, between the night staff's fifteen-minute checks, he had slipped away. She was managing to share the relief. For me, not surprise, but wonder.

And there is nothing, absolutely nothing to stop you, whoever you are reading this, to open your life to the angel energy. Stepping stone to Life, God, Goddess, Source, whatever your language may be, and to an increasing knowledge of the pure love that created the world and, often unheeded, is always there for you. Angel energy is so close to the Energy of Source that it never deviates from that creative Love.

But how do I start? How do I find everyday angels for me? Practical beginnings may come from the many angel books now available. Put in a request at the library and enjoy what comes for you. But this may be just 'reading about'—I want to go further. There are three attitudes that to me seem essential for the start of any angel exploration. They are: *stillness; joyful anticipation; trust.*

Strangely, these attitudes are sadly lacking in today's society. Recently a middle-aged couple bought the cottage next to me, very pleasant people. But I was horrified to discover they 'needed' their stereo on so loud that the music distorted, leaking through our thick stone walls. No more peace for me! The explanation was that if it wasn't so loud, they couldn't hear it all over the house! Later, decorating the bedroom, windows wide open, their radio blasted its way far down the village street. It is their second home so, perhaps thankfully for me, it is frequently empty, and at peace. But how sad, only to be safe with noise. Angels like *stillness*.

Joyful anticipation...I have used anticipation instead of expectation because we so often make expectation definitive. If I am to relate with an angel it must be...have...offer...? Not so, I just joyfully imagine something will happen, sight, scent, feeling, or a totally unknown factor. I am open to whatever the Ageless Spirit can offer. Very different to the presentation of today's media, politics, terrorism, which soon drops me into the trap of negative expectation.

And *trust*. These three qualities apply to all our inner journeying, not just in relation to angel energies. The more we journey, the more we know. But there is always more to discover. We need to trust that the journey is going well and will go further as we learn to live in the power of the Light. We need also, learning to live inside out, to lift some of this inner trust up into our sometimes trust-less outer lives. Truly the angels are there for us, just waiting for us to approach them. Believe it, trust, and go forward.

Practicalities: as a first step, practise stillness. Allow yourself five minutes just to sit, eyes closed, watching the rise and fall of your breathing. Thoughts will scurry past, no matter—let them come and go. They are only surface froth; go back to the breathing. It may help to *count* each in-breath, one to ten, then start again, over and over as the stillness deepens.

I have used my favourite stillness method for many years now. Here it is. Prepare first by turning off the phone, shutting the door, sitting comfortably and beginning once more to watch the breathing. But this time, right in front of you, imagine a large sheet on which two words are written, in light. The word LOVE is a beautiful rosy pink; beside it, the word PEACE is a deep indigo-violet. Now, in time with your breathing, silently read your words, LOVE as you breath in, PEACE as you breathe out—love, peace, love, peace, love, peace. Be aware that as you read, the actual energies are flowing through and round you. Breathe in the love energy, breathe it out as peace.

Practise this exercise for a few days, any time of day or night. You may use it to help you sleep, or for calm after anger, or to banish fear. Two or three times a day—stillness.

Then you are ready to go on. Before you journey into stillness, decide which everyday angel you would like to meet today? Your guiding angel, your guardian angel, or an angel who will help you in any aspect of your life—health, work, relationship, skills, strength, perseverance? Sit quietly and let some suggestion come to mind. Then on with the breathing, the love-peace energies and imagine yourself in a place you feel would be good for an angel meeting, a garden, a country setting, a beach, a well-known place, or some-where quite unknown to you as yet. Remember, the angel energy is pure Love—anticipate feeling this in some shape or form. Remain quiet, trust, and enjoy the experience.

Another preparation I enjoy is first to become still, then imagine yourself centred in a wonderful circle of the peace colour, indigo-violet, deep, still, comforting, a bit like being wrapped in velvet. The edge of the circle is shining gold, with light flying off into your sur-roundings. (This is a good one to use just in your ordinary living room.) Breathe the peace, soak in the colour, and when you are ready, ask an angel to visit you.

So you choose the place of the meeting, and can ask for whatever you want. Remember this is a relationship, so you need to give as well as receive. What can you give an angel? Thank-you is the basic gift, given in anticipation and trust, even before you know the result of your request. Trying to live always in love is another gift, keeping you close to the angel energy, in appreciation. You may want to have a special flowery oil burning or, if you have room, make a little corner welcoming for angel adventures, perhaps with candle or crystals, or even the lovely Woodstock angel models. Whatever you feel makes a welcome offering.

Some people set up quite a ritual of colour, light and sound. If this is right for you, then enjoy being creative in this way. But it is important to remember that there are no rules, each relationship is necessarily different, between two different beings. I tend only sometimes to use candles and find that out in the countryside the beauty and peace is already there and my angels and I can joyfully share it.

Ideas will come. I have never deliberately tried to create an angel, for keeping an open mind, they create pictures for me, as needed. One day, feeling totally isolated and alone, I just wanted someone to comfort me. What happened? The picture came to mind of an angel of tenderness. She was a very plump, almost voluptuous figure, half lying on a couch, and I found myself almost buried in her fulsome breasts as she cuddled me to her—child to archetypal mother. She is always around if I need her.

The third preparation is even simpler. You need to come to your angel meeting fresh and clean, the space around you the same, so that you do not blur the light in which angels travel. You may have heard the saying, 'Angels can fly because they are light.' When you are calm and still, imagine yourself filling up with light surrounding you, soaking into you. It need not be a harsh light, perhaps a gentle glow. Whatever you see is right for you, but be *aware* of the light—filling you and reaching out to meet that of your angel visitors. Some people may find it easier to use a definite system, light to feet, to legs, to abdomen and so on. Use this method if it feels right for you. Just let the light flow in.

How do you know if an angel is there? Like the little boy in the story, your heart will be the place of knowledge. Oh yes, there may be outward signs, a scent, a feeling, a picture, but inside it is just a visitation of Love. Some folk think that the appearance of a small white feather means there is an angel about. An amusing incident, here. When I was told of this, in my correspondence course, I went off to the arboretum which, as such a place of peace and beauty, would surely, I thought, welcome angels—and feathers. Sure enough, as I walked around, there it lay, a small soft patch of white, and a few feet on, another. Again and again—I stopped counting at forty. It was not a windy day, no dead birds about, and I have never seen such a widely spread display. Coincidence? Or another spiritual clue?

And, of course, nowadays there are many, many angel products. Be careful, let your intuition say yes to whatever you purchase—something that really speaks to you, really supports you on your journey. I enjoy angel cards, a pack describing every quality with accompanying angel on each card. Many uses, particularly; for me, a wonderful base for meditation. I keep mine in a little box on the mantelpiece and most days take out the card and ask for the angel quality I most need to contact today. Drawn out, I leave it on view, think about it, maybe feel it and let it speak to me in any way that happens. (A hint here, if you really don't like the one you choose—without looking—find out why. It might hold an important message.)

There is so much more. I am just offering you starters; yours may be different—that's fine. Your own angels are waiting to carry you on, spirit to Spirit . Approach them through stillness, with joyful anticipation and in the trust that deepens the further you travel. What a welcome as the energies meet!

6

DEATH—The Approach

The next two chapters, looking at the mystery of death, are going to start with a story, a story that I believe cuts across the usual divide between inner-outer, real-unreal, spiritual-material, and so brings life into synergy. How? Simple—it is fiction on one layer, deep life truths on another, melded into just one story.

This first chapter is to be about the travelling, the life journey which you might see, from an early age, as the long gradual approach to the life/death/life transformation which awaits us all. And here again we can use the 'stillness, joyful appreciation, trust' approach to carry us fearlessly forward. The second chapter moves on to the actual celebration as transformation takes place.

We are used to talking about death—if we dare—by trying, logically, to work out what may happen. Sometimes bits of hotly disputed 'evidence' appear, near-death experiences, spiritualist magic. All these merit discussion—books, logic, left of brain stuff. My hope is that this story will approach death in a very different way. Not logic, not human-type reason, but glimpses of reality gained through experience, intuition, trust, yes, and fantasy, for the right side of the brain to work on.

Just for a little while then, throw out fear, preconceived ideas, sit back open-mindedly, relax and enjoy as you read. It is only part of a much larger story (at both levels). I am sharing the section relevant to our exploration of the death journey.

The hero of this story is the boy Edrin, who lives in a small mountain community directed by a Council of Warlocks. Magic is commonplace, Love is considered the ruling energy, and the whole community lives under the unseen protection of the Great Creator, Master of the White Light.

Edrin is about to set out on a quest. He must travel to a far-off unknown destination, there to find a gift to bring back to the community. This task must be completed by Midsummer Day, his thirteenth birthday. If successful, he will then be eligible for acceptance as a full adult Warlock Councillor. If not, he must wait and try again the following year.

He has only two things to help him. Mordecai, his mentor and teacher, has given him a magic talisman, a shining stone with a hole in the middle. This, held up to the sun, can focus his intuition and so direct and strengthen him. His gentle earth-mother handed him a fine silver chain. 'Each link,' she said, 'is a gift of love, my love and Life-love. It will carry any weight you put on it. It will fasten anything you need to keep safe. It belonged to your grandmother, and her grandmother before her. Now it is for you and offers you the power of this line of wise women, whenever you should need it.' Now the magic stone sat safe on the chain—the chain round his neck. Thus connected to the two people he loved most in the world, Edrin set off on his long journey. He had only one instruction: 'As soon as the path turns, look low.'

He climbed and climbed, until the village was just a collection of black dots far below. His legs felt like jelly but he knew that at this stage magic would not help him. Up and up he went.

He hadn't noticed a turn in the path, but suddenly realised the sun was now on his left. 'Look low,' he remembered and dropped to his knees. Nothing, just the sparse grass at the edge of the path. Do I go on, or do I wait?

Suddenly he was aware he was being watched. He didn't feel anything threatening in the watching so, staying very still, he, in his turn, looked carefully around. Ah, two tiny black eyes shone in the glint of the magic stone. Peering out from under a large leaf they vanished as Edrin started to come forward. Quickly, he changed to thought power and froze just where he was. 'Have you got something to show me?' he thought. 'Please come out—I won't hurt you, whoever you are.'

A small head reappeared. Edrin could see it belonged to a minute mouse, so tiny it would have fitted neatly onto his own thumb. 'May I pick you up?' he thought. The mouse's whiskers twitched but he stayed still as Edrin gently placed him on the palm of his hand and brought him up to eye level. 'Please, can you help me?' said his thought, 'I am on a journey to find what I need before I can be accepted as a full warlock. I must be back by Midsummer's Day, but I don't even know what it is I am looking for. I was just told to climb the mountain and look low at the first bend in the path. And I found you.'

The tiny black eyes looked. They looked at the silver chain and they looked at the magic stone. Then they looked straight into Edrin's eyes. High-pitched, clear and bell-like came the mouse's thought-reply:

'You are looking for your great, great grandmother. It is nearly time for her to leave, but she is waiting to hand on to you the special wisdom you need.'

'Where do I go to find her?'

'Climb to the top of the mountain and when you see the view before you, hold out your stone and it will tell you what to do next.'

'Thank-you, oh thank-you. Is there something I can do for you?'

The little mouse looked bashful and turned its head away. Edrin waited. The bell-thought sounded again.

'When you have found your grandma, will you use your magic, think-stroke me and make me well?'

Edrin was about to say 'I know nothing about healing' but the mother-chain suddenly felt heavy about his neck. Understanding, he said, quietly, quietly, in his most gentle rose-coloured thought: 'Of course I will.' And it was strange, for as the little mouse scurried away he seemed almost to glow, surrounded by a soft rosy light.

Edrin followed the new path, which quickly circled round and brought him to the plateau at the top of the mountain. The breeze was so strong that he could hardly stand, and the view was so vast, he felt as though he could see the whole world. Where, in all that, could he hope to find his grandam?

Almost he panicked, but a little bell-like tinkle in his ear reminded him of the mouse's instruction. Taking the chain from his neck, he held the stone out at arm's length. Immediately there was a huge gust of wind, and a great burst of rain, hammering down till he could hardly breathe. But the sun shone beyond him and a vast rain-bow arched from the stone. Down and down it went and seemed to anchor again far, far away in a small patch of green at the centre of which was a tall building. *That* is where I must go next, he thought.

And so his journey began. It was filled with adventure. Though he travelled under the protection of the White Light, the Children of the Dark were always out to get him; they teased and tricked remorselessly. He was terrified on his first night on the mountain when, on waking, he thought at first he was surrounded by a circle of hostile people, jeering and threatening. How could he escape?

Then the oft-repeated advice of his mentor came to mind. 'In times of danger stop, be still, remember.' Remember? Suddenly Edrin did. There isn't anyone out there; it's the Children of the Dark practising their thought throwing. Relief flowed through him. Standing straight and tall, he stretched out his right hand and, turning sunwise, drew a full circle round himself. 'Within this circle I claim the protection of the Great Creator, Master of the Light.' For a moment he stood silent and then, with a great shout, said, 'Be gone, all ye of the dark!'

From the edge of his circle light flashed and shone. Just for a moment Edrin could clearly see the whole plateau, even far in the distance a glimpse of his destination. He could move on.

Another time, having crossed their path and refused their directions, two burly men appeared, picked him up and tossed him into a great bed of nettles. The nearer he came to the castle (for this the faraway building became) the more dangerous the threats became. The worst thing they did was to cause the loss of his talisman. A great bird came and plucked the chain from his outstretched hand as he held it up for further direction. Putting its great beak through the centre hole, it flew away, the chain dropping to the ground. Not all was lost. A small snake wriggled down the hillside and after a long search appeared triumphantly, carrying the chain round its neck. It had not forgotten Edrin's help for him a few days previously, soothing and healing his poor dried out cracked skin. 'But the talisman, how will I manage without it?' Edrin's thoughts buzzed like an angry bee.

Doggedly he plodded on, not forgetting his morning and evening meditation, and consulting his intuition as best as he could. If he began to feel lonely he sometimes spent time quietly bringing his mother to mind, his mentor too, and occasionally the bonny lass, Rowanna, who at home was his close friend and playmate. It felt like a conversation. He picked up their encouraging thoughts and it was easier, then, to continue.

Not all the adventures were bad. He travelled in trust and it was amazing how shelter for the night turned up at just the right moment. The little mountain hut, offering all necessary provisions, with a huge notice above the door saying, 'This hut welcomes all travellers to the mountain. Use what you need—take nothing away. Leave a gift. Sleep well.' Bliss! Edrin made a fire and in a little pan set two huge potatoes and two eggs to boil. Waiting for the food to cook he sat in the doorway and allowed his mind to flow free, just as he had been taught. He knew, even if he was not aware of anything happening, that these times of quiet free flow were what kept him in touch, in some inexplicable way, with the Great Master of the White Light. Every day…the thought thumped through his mind: 'Every day I must make space for this resting, this hidden meeting.'

The meal was cooked. Edrin filled the big tin plate with the potatoes, chopped the hot eggs among them, then sliced cheese on top. Oh, he was *so* hungry, it was so good. Settling down, he said the bedtime blessing he had so often heard from his earth mother at bedtime. 'From this house we send out love and light. May no darkness enter it this night.' And he was instantly asleep.

Early next morning he was up, chopping a huge pile of wood as his gift. But he wanted more, so, standing tall in the middle of the single room, he stretched out his arm and, slowly turning sunwise,

declared, 'Within this circle I claim for this hut the Power and Protection of the Great Creator. May it keep safe all travellers who rest
here and may no dark enter.' For a moment the whole place was lit
by a rosy glow. Edrin opened the door and walked out. As he did so
the rainbow appeared, arching from the door handle and away
down the mountain, once again indicating the right direction.

Many more stops, all interesting, all different. The farmer
enquired about his destination and then asked, 'Would you help
with the milking tonight? My lad's away ill.' Edrin hesitated. The
farmer took a huge key from the hook at the barn door. 'You can
have all the milk you want to drink and there's a little shed full of
clean straw where you can shelter.' He grinned, 'I'm nowt to do
with the Dark,' he said, 'but take the key and if you're affeared, lock
yourself in for the night.' Full of warm milk and a hefty sandwich
the farmer's wife brought out, Edrin slept heavily and was ready to
be off by daybreak.

Then there was dear old Jake, sitting quietly on the bench outside
his cottage, just needing to talk. Edrin stayed two nights here, mind-
ing Jake while his carer-grandaughter went off on the first whole day
out she had enjoyed for many years. And it was from Jake that he
heard the first news of his grandam. 'I met her once,' said the old
man. 'I was just a little lad. My grandfather used to work at the castle sometimes, leaving me to play on the hillside outside the castle
walls. One day a lady came to the gate and called me to her. "Are
you alright, my love?" she asked. "Your grandfather won't be long."
She gave me a big piece of bread, spread thick with wild raspberry
jam, and sat beside me while I ate. We looked at each other, and I
can hardly tell you how it was. Her eyes were a deep dark blue, and
as I looked into them everything shimmered and shook. I felt as if I

were inside a great warm cloud of light and loving. Everything *was* alright, very alright. I don't know how long we looked, but then she just laughed, patted me on the head and went in, leaving me to eat up my bread and jam. I felt different somehow, special and strong. I've always remembered her and wished I could look into those eyes again.'

Off he went to bed, early, so that he could lie and look out the window at the night. 'Aye,' said Jake, 'I watch the stars, and feel the breeze through the open window. I smell the flowers exercising their Spirit in the cool of the evening. There are always crumbs on the windowsill and small birds call in on their way to bed. It is sharing time. I lie, just thinking of the world with love, and all the life around me seems to join in, and think of me.'

As Edrin got nearer the castle there were more contacts with the life there. Late one afternoon he came to a clearing where a man was digging in a vegetable patch.

'Hello,' the man said, 'where are you off to?'

Edrin looked at him doubtfully. Was he of the Dark? They were so good at disguise. 'Oh, I'm just walking, and looking for a place to shelter for the night. It's too hot on the track'.

It was almost funny—it was the man's turn to look mistrustful. Nobody just walked around there. Was this a child of the Dark?

They stood and looked at each other silently until a cat sprang down from the garden wall and, purring, rubbed round Edrin's feet, then appeared to be playing with something, jumping about, batting the air.

'He's playing with a rainbow ball,' thought Edrin. 'Is this your cat?' he asked.

'My wife's, really, but when she's working at the castle he stays with me.'

'Working at the castle!' exclaimed Edrin. 'That's where I'm going. If only the Dark will let me. Oh, tell me all about it.'

And that was another night, warm and safe, and a big breakfast as well as the first evening meal. Josef was such a lovely ordinary man. He showed Edrin a picture of his wife, Hazel, a plain comely face, and yet there was something about her eyes, blue as the summer sky and holding within so many secrets, so much magic! Edrin wondered how these two, so different, could get on together.

Josef smiled. 'I know what you're thinking,' he said. 'I'm so ordinary and Hazel's so special. I used to think that. I daren't ask her to marry me. But one day she said to me, "Josef, I would so much like to be with you. Working with Madame, watching her heal, hearing her speak of strange and wonderful energies, I get too excited and too tired. I sometimes feel I might fly away and spin off somewhere among so much energy. But with you I feel safe and loved and ordinary again. I need this—you are my good earthing. May I be with you?"'

Josef suddenly looked shy and embarrassed. 'I could hardly believe it, but I took a deep breath and said, "Do you really mean this? Would you really marry me?" And she said, "YES." For me she is magic and wonder, but for her I am indeed her good earthing. Every weekend we are together here.'

And then it was time to go on. The castle was very near now, perhaps one long day's walk. Then there was the lake to circle, and the high hill on which the castle stood, to climb. Josef had warned him this next day would be very hot, the track very exposed. He made him carry an extra bottle of water, and told him to be very sure always to watch out for the Children of the Dark.

Josef was right. Edrin walked and walked, the track just a hard rutted path running through dry scorched grassland. As the afternoon wore on he decided he would have to turn off earlier than usual onto one of the little side paths, to find shade and also shelter for the night. But which path?

The answer came into his mind as a picture. With a smile he remembered the morning when, on opening his eyes after his morning meditation, he found himself within a pattern of rainbows. Some were circling round him, some spiralling to the sky and back, some spreading great sheets of colour all around. Then he laughed, for there among the rainbows, playing with a rainbow ball, was a small fluffy kitten. It was getting itself into such a tangle, and enjoying itself enormously. Suddenly it realised Edrin was watching and with one small paw batted the ball across to him. The purring rumbling thought that came with it quite clearly stated, 'For you.'

That was it, the rainbow again. The kitten playing with the rainbow ball, a new idea, and passing it on to him. A different kind of talisman? Edrin pondered: 'Nothing I can physically hold but, like the kitten, something I can use through my imagination! Is this wishful thinking, or will it work? I'll try it!'

Standing still, he closed his eyes and saw very clearly the ball of rainbow colours—had Josef's cat been reminding him? With an imaginary swing of his arm he threw it up, saying firmly, 'As you come down, travel along the path I need to take to find my resting place.' As he opened his eyes he thought he saw a rainbow flash and *there* it was, his rainbow ball rolling, bouncing, even flying along the track ahead.

It passed the first side path, then the second, but darted off along the third one. Edwin grinned. 'I got it right,' he said, and he set off again, making for the third trail himself. It was really only a path, leading away into the hills. As he got further along he began to get shade from the few trees at the path edge. Indeed, as the sun got lower, he at last began to feel comfortably cool. The rainbow ball flashed ahead of him, so he had no need to make any decision, just follow.

Then, as he walked, his rainbow was joined by others, great spirals twirling down through the sky, dancing round the rainbow ball, then flaring up and away into the distance, only to return and join the journey. Edrin stopped to watch. It was like a mammoth firework display, more beautiful than any he had seen before. What was going on?

Continuing, he rounded a corner and found he was approaching a strange little dwelling. He was not sure what it was made of, and it seemed like a sort of mixture of every simple dwelling he had heard of—igloo, tepee, cave dwelling. 'Yet it is so special,' he said to himself. 'It looks like a small dome on the ground, but somehow it has become the focus of this wonderful rainbow play. If this is a place where the colours of the White Light come to play, someone very wise, great, and powerful must live here. How can it welcome me? I am not even a full Warlock yet?'

Edrin felt shy and embarrassed. But the little rainbow ball had no such inhibitions—it rolled in through the open doorway, and vanished.

Timidly Edrin followed, peering through the opening. He was looking into a homely kitchen. There was a fireplace, a table, and two chairs, a big cupboard for crockery and a tiny meshed tin cupboard holding a few items of fresh food, fruit and vegetables.

Edrin was so busy exploring the kitchen that he nearly didn't notice the second door, opening into a tiny bedroom. A bed was pulled up to the open window and on it lay the oldest man Edrin had ever seen. He was lying peacefully propped up on several pillows, his long grey beard resting smoothly on the cover. His arms were also uncovered, so thin and fragile that they seemed only skin and bone. Indeed, his whole body barely lifted the bedclothes.

And he was fast asleep. Who is he? Why am I here? It felt as though there must be some special reason for his coming. But what? Edrin settled himself comfortably to wait and within the deep peace and quiet of the place found his mind automatically flowing free. It felt as though he was dancing among the colours that circled the room. Sometimes they settled into a figure of eight, enclosing him and the person on the bed. Sometimes they flowed out through the window, silently rising to circle high above the castle before returning to this tiny dwelling and its old, old occupant.

It was so still, so safe, so relaxing. It did not take long for Edrin himself to fall asleep.

7

DEATH—The Celebration

(So, as in our lives, Edrin, under the protection of the White light, has been travelling on a path of trust, learning to follow his intuition, depending on new instructions, usually by going into the stillness and letting his mind flow free, as we also are learning to do. Now he approaches the greatest adventure of the whole quest.)

◆   ◆   ◆

He woke to find a pair of violet coloured eyes regarding him intently. The old man had turned his head on the pillow to get a clearer view of this grubby dishevelled young visitor. The expression now on his face was one of great kindness.

'Oh sire,' Edrin jumped to his feet. 'I am so sorry. I was just waiting quietly till you woke and the colours…I must have fallen asleep. Can I do something for you? Do you need a drink? Can I fetch something? Can I make you more comfortable?'

The low quiet voice cut across Edrin's babbling. 'It's alright, Edrin' (How does he know my name? Edrin thought), 'it was good to share sleep. I have been waiting for you for so long. It was right for us to be tired together. But I think it must be you who has needs just now. Are you not hungry? My good neighbour visits me each morning, leaves food and pumps more water. Look in the cupboard and find yourself something to eat and drink.'

'What about you? Let me see to you first.' Edrin plumped up the pillows and lifted the old man into a more comfortable position. He did not use the stale warm water, but went out to the pump, returning with a mug of the clear cold drink. 'There,' he said, 'and what would you like to eat?'

'No,' replied the old man, 'I don't eat much now. The water is energised for me and is enough. Make yourself something and take it outside to eat. I will rest here and look at the castle. See how its windows glaze in the setting sun?' His face changed as he looked, some deep satisfaction showing in his smile.

When Edrin had finished his meal he came in to see that all was well. The old man looked much more vital now, and patted the bedcover. 'Come and sit near me,' he commanded. 'We will talk for a little while in the cool of the evening.'

There was a long silence. The breeze fluttered the curtains and stirred soft tendrils of the old man's beard. Edrin waited. At last he spoke. 'My name is Jedorah, and I have lived a very long life this time. I have travelled the world and met many people also travelling in the Light. We shared wisdom and healing and encouraged each other when the Dark was about, threatening our individual journeys. For this life I chose usually to be alone, to be free for other people, and I have not recently been in touch with the Warlock Council. You will find, nevertheless, that they know me well. Years ago I was Chief Warlock and nurtured many a lad like yourself. Your Mordecai was one of my students. I remember clearly the scrapes he got into as he completed his first quest.'

Edrin giggled as he tried to picture his grave stern tutor as a mischievous little lad.

The old man continued: 'Many lives ago, when I was still a young soul, I lived a life with my soulmate. I was strong and handsome then—dark curls like yours. She was beautiful, slim and strong, hair piled up on her head yet escaping to her waist. We loved each other so much, and grew together in love and healing. We knew, too, that we might not always be together. She left before I did, that time, and the sadness was huge.

'Since then, sometimes she has been in a life when I have not, and I have been her spirit guide. Sometimes she has done this for me. Occasionally we have had glimpses of each other, on one life or another as we worked hard to complete the particular birth vision we had chosen for that time.

'This time, as my body became fragile, and this life's active work drew to a close, I built this little dwelling where I could rest and watch over her dwelling as we waited to leave.' His old eyes softened as he looked at the castle.

Edrin gazed at him in amazement. 'You are saying that great, great grandam is your love, your soulmate?'

'I am. And we are sharing this last task together. I had expected to leave years ago, as my body got old and tired. Then you were born and I knew I had to wait till you were ready to visit me, and share some of the ancient wisdom I am holding for you. Your grandam is the same, waiting to teach and share with you. But when this last task is complete, then we can leave. Because of you we have a chance to meet and be together as we go through the deathgate and are again at home.' The old man's face lit up at the thought. Edrin could hardly take it all in. Soulmates, birth visions, life tasks, death-gates…Mordecai had taught him a great deal about travelling in the Light, about white magic, about the Children of the Dark and their tricks and dangers. But what Jedorah was telling him was somehow more personal, deeper and both frightening and encouraging. His thoughts chased each other round in a kind of fog.

'Time to rest now. If you will see to my needs and make me comfortable, we can talk again in the morning. I have one special lesson for you to learn, among all the other wisdom that is here for you. I think it is not for tomorrow. There is time for you to stay for a while and still have time for you to complete your journey.'

Edrin made the old man comfortable; then, picking up a rug and cushion, settled himself at the open doorway and quickly fell asleep. Unknown to him, the colours settled in a safe spiral round the dwelling, its point raising high into the sky. While far, far above, a huge white bird circled in silent satisfaction before flying home for the night.

It was early in the morning when Edrin was woken by the sun as it crept out from behind the castle to shine in his eyes. He sat up and looked around him. It was so quiet. The castle towered above, and the small lake glinted in the early sun. Birds were about and, undisturbed, rabbits and other small creatures played on the grass at the lakeside.

Edrin felt refreshed and clear. He would have liked to set out now, in the cool of the early morning, to finish his journey, to walk round the lake and climb the steep path to the castle. But Jedorah had been quite sure he had time to stay awhile. Edrin felt in the secret pocket of his shorts and made another notch in his time-stick. Six nights gone now. How long would Jedorah expect him to stay?

'Trust,' he said to himself, 'I must stop worrying and trust. How can things go wrong when a great master like Jedorah promises to teach me more of the ancient wisdom? And my grandam wants to do the same.' Leaning back against the doorpost, Edrin began his morning meditation, breathing calm and relaxed, mind allowed to float free. He had made no special request, but almost as soon as his eyes were closed, pictures formed inside them.

It seemed that he and Jedorah were leaving the dwelling and walking along a gently spiralling path. It was quite smooth and wide, but also steadily climbing to its destination. The old man was getting very tired.

'Shall we turn back?' asked the boy.

'No,' gasped Jedorah, breathing now with difficulty. 'It is my time now. It is not far, if you will help me.'

Edrin put his arm round the old man and half walking, half being carried, Jedorah continued on the way.

Then, as they rounded a bend in the spiralling path, they came to a gate, right across the path. It was an amazing gate. Edrin was not sure what it was made of, but it was patterned in the most delicate way, holding many images, of animals, fish, flowers and birds. There was the sun, and the moon and stars. There were waves from the sea, small waterfalls and fountains from the streams and rivers. Edrin blinked. For as he looked, sometimes it looked like an ordinary gate, sometimes everything seemed alive and moving.

There was no way of going through, for the gate was locked and chained. Jedorah was content just to lean on it and rest.

'Where does the path go?' asked Edrin, for the view on the other side was blurred and misty. 'Are you strong enough to go on?'

In his dream, Jedorah turned and looked at him. 'Don't you know?' he asked. 'This is the deathgate. Isn't it beautiful? They will come soon and open it. I want you to stay and watch me go through. It will be so wonderful.'

Edrin's breathing started to race. It was so real and so strange. He was glad to open his eyes. There was his backpack on the grass beside him, and the ordinary doorpost supporting him. Looking through the open doorway he could see Jedorah, very much alive, stirring in his bed. Edrin rushed to him.

'I had such a strange meditation,' he said,'or was it a dream? I really, really thought you were dying. Oh, I'm so glad you are here and we can talk.'

'Tell me about it after breakfast. I would like a little bread and fruit today. Come in and eat with me. Sit on the windowsill, then I can watch you and the castle at the same time.'

He must be feeling better if he is eating, thought Edrin. Carefully he prepared breakfast for them both. It felt like a celebration as they quietly ate and drank while shifting strands of sunlight spilled into the room.

'I wonder,' he thought, 'if I carried the big chair out, would Jedorah like to be in the fresh air and the sun?'

Before he could ask, though no words were spoken, the reply came. 'Lovely, get it ready and carry me out. I haven't been out for weeks now. The big tree will give plenty of shade.'

In a very short time they were settled. The tree welcomed them as Edrin carried Jedorah out, piled up the cushions and made him comfortable.

'You need the rug too,' he said. 'There, is that right for you?'

The old man leaned back. 'It is wonderful,' he said, 'to see the castle and the lake and feel the breeze, and have the sun warm on my feet—and to have you here at last. I will rest for a while now, and later we can talk.'

He slept nearly all morning. Edrin washed their few dishes, shook out the bedclothes, drew water from the well, even entertained a visitor. This was the friendly neighbour, a plump homely woman, carrying eggs and a newly baked loaf of bread.

'He will be so pleased you are here,' she said. 'He has been expecting you for days. It seemed very important to him. I am glad, too. I hated to think of him alone all day. Can you stay for a while?'

'I am going tomorrow,' replied Edrin, 'but not first thing. Perhaps you could come a little later to see that all is well?'

'I'll come after lunch. I'll not disturb him now. Tell him I called and how glad I was to see that he was so well looked after.' And she bustled away.

'Why did I say I was going tomorrow?' Edrin asked himself. 'I promised Jedorah I'd stay as long as he needed me. Oh well, I can always change my mind.' He looked over at the figure resting peacefully under the tree. 'I really love him,' he thought. 'How strange, and I've only known him for one day. Somehow we belong together.' He went out and sat down close to this fragile figure of power, and at once knew what Jedorah was thinking.

'I am not going to talk much today, lad,' the old man said softly. 'I am tired, and being together will be enough. Our energies mingle and the Love of the White Light welds us together. At your meditation time, I told you what was going to happen tonight. It was good that you heard me, even though you called it a dream. You know now that it is tonight that I leave, so you are free to go on tomorrow. We have the rest of the day to share thoughts. You do this often with the little animals and with your homefolk. So just sit quietly now and listen to my teaching. Close your eyes if you like, rest against me, take one of my hands in your own. Do not struggle to remember what I say. It will all come back when you need it.'

Time stood still. Or perhaps it galloped away. Edrin opened his eyes again to see the sun once more sending an evening light to shine on the castle windows. He couldn't have told Jedorah what he had heard and understood, but he felt different. His hands, still cupping Jedorah's, were hot and tingling and almost all of him felt fiercely alive.

Jedorah was looking at him. 'I think it's time we went in,' he said. 'Time to get ready for your task with me. Are you afraid of accompanying me to the deathgate?'

Edrin thought for a while. 'If you had asked me that this morning I would have said yes, but things have changed.'

'Tell me what you understand now.'

'I know that the spirit inside you is strong and beautiful, powerful and loving. I know too that all these later years it has had to work through a body that is getting weaker and weaker. Now it longs to be free, to go home. It will leave your bodyshell empty at the deathgate. It will float free, fly forward—no more pain, fragility, exhaustion. I know that it has been held prisoner longer because you waited for me. I shall be glad to come with you to the place of your release.'

He picked up the fragile old body and placed Jedorah comfortably in the remade bed. The castle glowed red now, in the sunset, and Edrin knew Jedorah was quietly saying goodbye to the grandam who was also watching, to see him leave. For a few minutes he left them together, himself sitting again at the door, eating some of the new bread, spread thickly with the neighbour's wild raspberry jam

'Will you share my bed tonight, lad?' asked Jedorah as he came in. 'I would like to hold you for a while. Just lie on top of the quilt, use the rug if you are chilled.'

It felt very special. Jedorah's arm came round Edrin and they lay without speaking, Edrin sharing the rhythm of the old man's breathing. Something was happening again—energy flowed, heart to heart, breath to breath. Edrin felt as though for the first time he was a part of the whole universe, flowing together, no division of shape or form. The sky breathed with him, the sun shared its light, the mountain's rhythm shook deeply beneath them. Every part of the life was there, while Jedorah's old heart kept the beat.

Warn out, his own arm crept over Jedorah's weightless body, his head drooped against the old shoulder. Edrin slept.

◆   ◆   ◆

He was woken by singing, a song he had never heard before. It was very quiet and very beautiful and as he listened he could recognise the source of many of the sounds. There was a high note, coming he knew from the mouse-life, a slithery snake sound like the note of a violin, a deep rumbling bass from the mountain, even his own sound, soaring in sweet melody. The belonging feeling that had welcomed Edrin in sleep increased now as he listened, awestruck, to what he thought must surely be the very soul of the universe singing.

The song changed after a while, to a sort of plaintive calling. Edrin opened his eyes to see there the now familiar dance of the rainbow colours. But there was scent too. The flower spirits were offering their contribution: heather, honeysuckle, jasmine, rose, pouring it out in wild abandon. It was a celebration, no doubt about that.

Then, within the circle of the rainbow, Edrin could just make out hazy figures shining. They had come to open the deathgate and fetch the master, he realised. He was right, it was wonderful. As the thought travelled through his mind, Jedorah's arm gave him a gentle hug, then dropped quietly onto the bed. At the same time the room was filled with White Light, so intense Edrin had to close his eyes. The singing, sung by the immense life choir, rose to a huge crescendo, and perfume washed over him in waves, every flower he had ever known, and more besides. What a celebration!

Gradually, gradually, everything reverted to the everyday of life. Wishing he had not to see, Edrin opened his eyes, sat up, and looked at the bodyshell from which so recently Jedorah had gone. The blue eyes were still open, and as he had been told, Edrin gently closed them. 'You have no need to look at the castle now,' he said. 'Your spirit can be there as often as you wish, while you wait for her to join you.'

He looked at the old, old face. It was so peaceful. The lines and wrinkles still demonstrated some of the hard old life that had been lived, but the expression was of total contentment, no, further, that of delight. Edrin folded the two old hands on Jedorah's chest, smoothed the grey beard for the last time, and straightened the quilt. 'There,' he said, 'they will come and see to your bodyshell later, and place it under the tree, as you wished. Perhaps, with Grandam. I shall be able to watch, from the castle, and say another goodbye.' He bent over and kissed the wise old forehead. There was a tingle of energy there for him. 'Goodbye,' he said, 'and thank you.' It all felt very flat now, and lonely. It was strange getting ready to go in the emptiness of the little dwelling. Edrin filled his water bottles, took some fruit, and for the last time in this refuge, sat down to let his mind flow free. 'I WILL get to the castle,' he promised. 'I WILL.' But nothing happened. It seemed at first as though the Light and the colours had gone. A tremor of fear shivered through Edrin's body, but he persevered. 'O Great Creator, Master of the White Light, I thank you for bringing me so far in safety. For allowing me to be with Jedorah as he was welcomed home. Now I am alone again, please guide me safely through this last bit of the journey.'

He waited, breathing quietly and trusting. Waves of a wonderful deep dark velvet-blue peace and calm gradually surrounded him. He felt totally protected and held, and the circle of gold, edging the blue, defied any infiltration by those of the Dark. That was not all for, strangely, it seemed that just then a firm hand grasped his shoulder (was it Jedorah?) and he heard, 'Trust and all will be well.'

It was time to move on. Edrin picked up his bag and, with one last unbelieving look at this so plain small dwelling within which such vast and wonderful energies had shown themselves, he set off toward the main track, the lake and the castle.

◆   ◆   ◆

So that is the story, and I expect you will have realised that as well as being a tale of a lad travelling on a quest, it is also the story of you and me, travelling on the inner journey. Make time sometime, in a quiet space, to read the story again, this time being Edrin, sharing his experiences and recognising very similar ones of your own, from your very different mode of travel.

For the inner journey, in one sense, is not about striving to reach a goal—that is not so important. What matters is, like Edrin, steadily, even doggedly sometimes, to keep travelling. And in the travelling learning from all our life experiences, changing our life perspective as we go. Yes, and this means even in old age too—keep travelling, keep learning, and most of all, keep in the Ageless Spirit Love-flow, to have and to give, to know and to share.

And increasingly, as we travel, we begin truly to understand that all life flows in this one Energy. That the birds, insects, beasts, flowers, sun, wind and rain contain the same Ageless Spirit that has flowed through us, in this human life, from the time our first two cells came together at conception. We find that we hold within ourselves endless potential, to be uncovered as our awareness grows. Learning to trust intuition, to appreciate healing, to share with others, all other life forms, with love, all that comes our way. To jettison the belief in 'coincidence', instead happily welcoming these sudden junctionings of inner and outer energies as clues to our journeying further, in and on.

And then the death experience, just a corollary really to what we have learned. Just now I have a human body, then I shall no longer have a human body, but the 'I' that is my share in the Ageless Spirit as it flows on. None of us knows exactly how this will be. And as each human being is different (and isn't that a miracle?) so each may have a different journey through the deathgate. No matter, the same flow carries us through.

We see so many examples of the life/death/life continuum in our daily life. I visit the arboretum now, in the winter, and it is so quiet as to be almost eerie, and my small dog sticks to my feet. Everything is 'dead' and I suddenly realised that all the trees were travelling deep inside, in this 'death' space, ready for the next surge forward. When I looked more closely, it had started, great fat buds waiting quietly for the time to move on. Your experience? Mine?

You must, in your long life, have had many such experiences? An episode that ended, apparently finally. Loss of a friend, a partner's death, an inevitable apparently diminishing change of lifestyle, a disability or other serious health loss—fill in your own life experiences. And yet, and yet, the flow didn't stop. Perhaps very slowly, perhaps surprisingly quickly, new experiences came along, filtered in, and changed everything. That is *if you had courage and did not try to stop the flow.*

So why do we feel so afraid of death—another life/death/life experience? Is it the unknown? Is it because we choose to deny the reality of the Ageless Spirit? Take time in your life now to watch how the world works on an endless pattern of life/death/life. Why should this be any different? Ask, in your meditation, and TRUST. As with Edrin, 'All will be well.'

I think any of these deaths, especially the apparently final one, can offer us spiritual clues and deeper understanding. It is as if, in our vulnerability and grief, we are open to inner touch. I have an indelible memory of the day my first, nine-day-old grandchild died from a hospital infection. They understood, at that hospital, how to help. First it was mugs of tea, and then they took us into a little treatment room where we could see him again. He looked sweet, fast asleep, with little blue lips. All three of us just stood and gazed. Back came Sister, asking his mother, 'Have you held him? You must say goodbye.' In turn we cuddled him and I found myself gently rocking him, while trickles of energy still flowed through. Not quite gone yet. What a short life visit, what a huge lesson about grief and letting go and…for me, about continuum. Some of his energy remains in my mind, a man now, and still my grandson. Nine days there, yet a potent bundle of Ageless Spirit, for what an amazing amount of love he drew to us, as others shared our grief.

Very different, some years later, when my ex-husband was terminally ill, and in a hospice near one of our children. I had been thinking about him when I went to bed, and at 1 a.m. I was woken up, very aware that he was there. Nothing to see, but absolute certainty of his presence. He had come to say goodbye, and all the rancour and sadness of our failed marriage had gone. It was a feeling of pure love. I heard myself saying 'Goodbye, sweetheart', a phrase I would never have used in the marriage, but a wonderful ending to a turbulent relationship.

My daughter rang me in the morning, to tell me he had died. 'I know, he came to say goodbye.' And it felt as though this ending was a special gift, an affirmation of Life-Love that left us both free to go on.

To finish on a lighter note, back to Edrin's story. I find this story is a great comfort when I start to divert from the inner journey. Perhaps I don't persist with daily meditation. Perhaps I insist on separatism. Perhaps I lose touch with my Spirit energy and with it lose compassion and care for those around me. Then, instead of beating myself up and feeling guilty and a failure, I just declare, 'Those wretched Children of the Dark, they're at me again! Banishing them, calling in the Light, I can make a fresh start.'

8

HEALING

Have you noticed that the different chapter headings of this book are virtually interchangeable, only a slight shift of emphasis calling out one title rather than another? So Magic includes Communication, Communication relationship, Energies all three, and so on. Isn't this exactly what life is all about? Synthesis, interchange, fostered and strengthened through the Ageless Spirit, which is our true be-ing? And healing, channelling of healing energies, seems to me to be a direct gift from this Life-Love, its expression very clear, very consistent, very recognisable. So, let's go on and explore it further.

What exactly do we mean by 'healing'? I suspect that for many people it means reduction of symptoms. Also, that it is more comfortable if contained within a system. So the complementary medicine treatments: aromatherapy, homoeopathy, reflexology, osteopathy, etc., are respectable pursuits. Even Reiki, the latest healing system, is now acceptable. But just 'healing' brings in a trickle of suspicion, even fear. Might it indicate treatment from charlatans, quacks and tricksters? Has the indicated healer got qualifications, certificates, is it safe, is it genuine, is it risky?

Over the years I have collected a clutch of definitions. Each gives one aspect of our understanding.

Healing is restoration of harmony: body, mind and spirit.

Healing is about right relationship: with you, with all life forms, within the universe and beyond, but especially with myself.

To love someone is to affirm them; to heal someone is to affirm them in their wholeness.

AND

Healing is just letting go into LOVE.

And here we discover that the Ageless Spirit flowing quietly through so many facets of life, carrying the love energy we so often cannot recognise, accept, or share, necessarily—within this flow—carries healing.

Over the years I have trained in several of the healing systems: radionics, colour, hypnosis…and also been the recipient of these and more. Gradually I have discovered that the system is really only a focal point, perhaps a comforting definite reassurance. What is important is the 'magic' behind it. We'll talk about that in a moment.

Years ago, completely new to any concepts of healing, I travelled to London to my first tutor, ostensibly to master the radionics system. When I reached her house I found she was still busy with her last patient, who lay comfortably on a couch in her bay window. She explained to me that she had been using colour healing. Blankly I looked around—no lamps, slides, pictures, no sign of colour. 'Mental colour healing,' she told me, 'received in your mind and shared in energy through your hands.'

This was the beginning of a learning situation for me that is clear now, thirty years later. This woman, a little dumpy 80-year-old with a mass of grey curls, had deep brown eyes. When she focused on you it felt as though you were stripped down to the deep and wonderful essentials you didn't know you possessed. It is impossible to describe how it felt when, lying on her couch, you felt colour washing through you, vivifying or calming, as appropriate. Centred, strengthened, and indeed moving to wholeness.

Her inner knowledge was very great, but she remained completely down to earth, and was continually giving me useful hints as my training continued. She was also completely remorseless if I did not listen and change!

'Stop doing all that thinking,' she said. 'Healing is not logic to be worked out. USE YOUR INTUITION.'

Soon after I began, she vetoed reading for a month. I looked at her in horror.

'Can't I even read a light book?' I asked.

'Oh well, a detective story, or something like that. But you are so busy searching, working out, making sense. Your brain is tired out, let it rest, trust your intuition to tell you what you need.'

And I did—and it did.

One more advice I have always followed—the magic.

'Sometimes you will need to refer a patient to another practitioner, chiropractor or osteopath perhaps. Always, of course, choose a good technician, but only choose one with that extra magic.'

She could have said, 'Someone who is closely in touch with the Ageless Spirit, and channels that power in healing.'

This advice I have always followed and was surprised to be caught out only recently when my own osteopath was away. In an acute state I had to take the only other practitioner available. He didn't have the magic. An excellent technician, but logic instead of intuition, and no sign of Spirit-love filtering through the touch. I cancelled my second appointment and waited for my magic lady. Who is, of course, a healer.

I think our concept of healing is often diminished because we see it as something too big. It happens again when we see it too small! I'll explain. It takes me back about thirty years when, in London, I attended my first transpersonal workshop. Coincidence, this? Having seen a short article on Transpersonal Psychology in the *Guardian*, a few days later at a New Year's Eve party, I asked a complete stranger what her work was! She was training to be a counsellor in the Transpersonal ethos. She told me more and sent me the invitation to the workshop.

On the first evening a group of us sat round in a circle and in turn gave our names, and what we did. One man just quietly said, 'I'm a healer.' I remember how amazing that seemed to me. What a gift, how wonderful, how lucky he was to be able to do something like that! I felt quite awestruck.

Ignorance? Superstition? Or perhaps a glimpse of the Ageless Spirit he was carrying? I was making it far too big, for I was drawing a firm line between him—so wonderful, and you and me—so ordinary. We are all healers. This I know, and suspect that small animals, birds, flowers, even the sun, rain and wind are healers too. Does your dog not lick you better if you are sad, and your cat give you peace and calm as she sits quietly on your lap with a roaring purr?

One of the first questions I am asked at a healing workshop: 'Can everybody heal?' The answer has to be 'Yes'—for life is geared, from most basic levels, to growth and wholeness. A surgeon can chop you up, remove the bad bits, stitch you up again. But he can't make the wound heal—life does that. Look back on your long life and remember times you have been a healer. No healer can 'do' healing, so take that out of your concept. A healer acts as channel, directing the healing to flow specifically to the needed place or person. A toddler falls down and starts to scream. Haven't you picked her up, rubbed the sore places, kissed her better? That's healing. Someone loses a much-loved partner. This is embarrassing, frightening for friends and acquaintances who cross the street because 'I don't know what to say'. Haven't you stayed with someone like that, listened, perhaps touched or held, been there for him or her? That's healing. Have you not written letters, made phone calls as continuance of contact for a lonely person? That's healing. Something as small as a smile, a cup of tea, a reassurance—that's healing.

What I am saying really is that every time you forget your *self* and open to let the Ageless Spirit Love be demonstrated, through you, then there are no boundaries, limitations definitions—just healing. And the other polarity, seeing actions as too small. The smile, the touch, the cuddles, such *little* things? No, not really. Channels for the greatest love of all—don't underestimate.

In this chapter I am going to share with you some of the healing experiences I was given in my years of working as healer/counsellor. Such different experiences, with a variety of people, but always a commonality, 'letting go into love.' And I realise now that the three attitudes I described as the means of approaching angels are also those needed as one opens to channel healing—stillness, joyful anticipation, trust. Part of the healing process is just to share those attitudes with the recipient. And to understand that the anticipation rests on the saying 'YES' to whatever the healing brings. Anything may happen and the joyful surprises are wonderful. Also, sharing Life-Love means just that—it goes out, it comes back. I got huge benefit by being given trust and comment from clients, and learned so much about life and courage, and sheer dogged holding on and moving forward.

I had an amusing and sobering grounding from one quite well known healer who rang to say 'thank you' for help I had given to one of her relations. Quite genuinely, I answered: 'Well, it wasn't really anything to do with me, I was just passing it on.' A mighty blitz came over the phone: 'How dare you say that! Do you really believe that channelling through a sewer is the same as through a clean pipe? Take on your part of the responsibility.' Gulp!

But I did say to aspiring healers: 'Think about it. If you really decide to be a healer, your life will change. How? You will begin to see life differently. For if you are constantly turning to the Source of all Love, then anti-love qualities and happenings will become impossible for you. In fact, you will be governed by a new morality. Not rules and regulations, just measured, sometimes censored, by love.' Not as impossible as it sounds—remember, you are Ageless Spirit, in spite of all the outer shell conflicts.

So who do I remember of the people who came? I'll try to give you a cross section. The strangest, perhaps most memorable was a healing session with a mouse. At that time I was a member of a weekly meditation group. The woman who acted as hostess had set up a very beautiful quiet meditation room, candles, crystals, sometimes quiet music. There were seven or eight of us, and we took it in turns to lead the meditation. I found it a little bit emotionally biased, and disliked going round the group afterwards with 'What did you get?' Meditation, to me, was about the going in. Still, as we chomped biscuits afterwards, there was good conversation and we all, though in different ways, shared the spiritual search.

One member of the group I held in deep respect. She owned an antique shop in town and was up at 5.30 a.m. to jog on the beach while sending out absent healing. If you looked into the shop and she thought you looked weary, she'd ask, 'Would you like some healing?' Upstairs, in a messy crowded storeroom, she sat you on a stool, standing behind you to provide a back. Ten minutes later you came out renewed and powerful.

This particular evening she was, very unusually, late. So we sat waiting. Suddenly she ran up the stairs, stuck her head in the door and said, 'Dorothy, will you come?' Surprised, I followed her down as she explained. 'I saw a cat torturing a mouse as I drove up. I rescued the mouse but I don't like handling them. Would you deal with it?' She opened the car door and there on the front seat lay this pitiable little creature. Totally traumatised, only its eyes flickered as I gently picked it up and for a moment or two held it cupped between my hands and gave it healing. It was so far gone that we decided the kindest thing to do would be to wrap it up and leave it on the seat to die in peace.

Back to the meditation room, we explained what had happened, and the real business of the evening began. It was a very convoluted meditation, the leader just back from a meditation course, and full of stories of temples, gardens, mountains. Somehow, I couldn't concentrate, so just stayed quiet, eyes closed. Then, to my amazement, all I could see, in my mind's eye, were my hands holding the little mouse, and shining on the mouse an absolutely beautiful blue light. I was fascinated and stayed watching until the 'What did you get?' question started round the circle. When it came to me, I apologised and said I hadn't been able to concentrate. Two seats further round my friend said, 'I didn't follow the meditation either; all I could see were Dorothy's hands holding the mouse, with an amazing blue light shining down on it.'

'*I* saw that!' I exclaimed, and we dashed out of the room, down the stairs, and to the car. On the seat lay the clean yellow duster. No mouse. Healed, it had gone home.

Another mouse healing, not so dramatic, but equally effective. I came out in the garden one afternoon and saw the body of a tiny mouse lying in the middle of the lawn. Intending to toss it in the field, I went to fetch the shovel, but as the shovel touched it, it moved. Looking closely, I saw marks of the cat on its back, but no broken skin. What to do? I thought of wrapping it up snugly in a box, in the house, but felt this might be even more terrifying. Fetching Rescue Remedy, I dropped this lavishly on its little head, held it for healing for a minute or two and then tucked it away, safe from marauders, in the middle of the dry stone wall surrounding the garden. Going out that evening, I peeped in to see if it was still alive. What a pathetic sight! Cold and shocked, it was lying there shivering and shaking, its little legs in perpetual motion. Back in the house I found some cotton wool balls, and after another showering with Rescue Remedy made a little nest in the wall and tucked the wee mouse in for the night. When I came home late I hadn't the heart to look again, but first thing next morning I peeped in. There were the cotton wool balls, nest almost undisturbed, and the mouse? Healed, it too had gone home! It was interesting that the healing energy of flowers (R.R.) as well as energy through my hands, had contributed to his unexpected recovery.

One more animal story which, at the time, was quite startling. My neighbours had two cats, a tabby, and a ginger one call TC (Top Cat). TC was incredibly shy. If anyone came to the house he quickly vanished out the back. I was no different from anyone else. But one morning, when my friends came downstairs, there was TC stretched out on the floor, obviously very ill. New to the area, they came in to me to ask about a vet, and promptly went off, with TC, to get help. While they were away I sat down and sent him absent healing. I was told he was responding well to the vet's treatment, and a couple of days later popped in to see how he was getting on. A small head peered round the door and then, to our stunned amazement, TC calmly walked across the room and, with a roaring purr, rubbed round my ankles. He knew!

Children are much the same. I found that when babies I had treated absently were brought to see me, they knew me and were glad to settle on my lap. Astonished parents commented, 'But he won't go to strangers!' We had connected, in energy terms, and they knew they were safe with me.

When and why do adults lose this sensitivity? Birds, beasts, flowers, children still understand the oneness of life, sharing, healing, loving. It seems that as adults we just focus on our separate—so obviously separate—parcels of skin and bone and have to start painfully to recognise again the unity in which we really belong.

I am often asked if all the people who come to me are on the spiritual search? The answer is, 'Yes, but not necessarily consciously.' The Ancient Wisdom instructs healers that they must start from where the patient is on the spiritual journey. To find this out is not always easy. Certainly no wise lectures or dishing out of inner information, as you yourself see it, just a hint or two thrown out and if taken up...Personally, I think this is not at all to do with words. If the healer travels as far as he/she can into his own healing space and expects to take the client with him, then this happens, and something changes. Always, of course, with the joyful anticipation.

I had a wonderful and amusing series of sessions with a teenage boy. The mother rang to tell me that her fifteen-year-old son was proud of his head of long blond hair, worn shoulder length. At least, *had* been, for now it was coming out in handfuls. He looked a mess, wouldn't go to school because the dinner ladies made fun of him, and was becoming increasingly suicidal. Could I help?

'Does he *want* to come?'

'He'll try anything. The consultant had said it was only a temporary condition, in three years he should be back to normal.'

Three years! At fifteen!

So we arranged that he should visit and see how I worked. If he then decided to continue, fine. I have to admit, with shame, that my heart sank as I looked out the window and saw this tall youth slouching up the path, misery and rebellion etched on his face. I was so wrong, for it soon became apparent that he had a wicked sense of humour. I ended up teasing him and we were both soon helpless with laughter. But the condition was serious enough and after a while I asked him if he would like me to give his head some healing energy.

'You may feel warmth, or tingling, or nothing at all. It certainly won't hurt.'

I didn't feel lying on a couch was suitable for this lad, so sat him in a chair, stood behind him, and after taking him into a relaxation put my hands gently on his head. I could feel my hands tingling violently as the energy flowed through, but he never moved or spoke, sitting remarkably at ease and relaxed. Finally I asked, 'Did you feel anything?'

'Oh yes,' he replied, 'it was like having sunshine, or a hot bottle, a lovely comforting warmth.'

'Good,' I said, 'that's all I'm doing today. Would you like to come back next week for more? Or think about it and give me a ring?'

'Oh no,' he said. 'I want to come back.'

So we fixed a date and a week later, back he came.

He still wasn't going to school and we had a long talk about this. He knew exactly what his life work was to be. He wanted to be a cabinetmaker and had already fixed up an initial apprenticeship with a local joiner.

'It's such a waste of time going to school,' he said. 'It's my O-level year and my mum's going crazy, but to me it's just stupid stuff and no use at all.'

'I see your point, it doesn't seem important. The only thing is, it's just possible that at some later date, when two of you are going for a job, they might say, in comparison, "Oh well, at least this lad stuck it out at school and got his O-levels. He's dependable, we'll choose him." But it's your decision and I do hear what you're saying.'

Hands on his head, I suddenly felt I should talk to him a little about spiritual energy. So I just said, 'This energy you can feel isn't really mine, it's just flowing through me. It comes from a much bigger energy; you might call it God or Spirit, or whatever.' Then, very tentatively, 'Do you have any ideas about that?' And that lovely boy said, 'I sometimes look up at the stars at night and I think, "Who made them?"' Then, after a pause: 'And then I think, "Who made *Him*?"'

He came once more, a fortnight later. He had gone back to school, wasn't standing any nonsense from the dinner ladies, was holding his shaggy head up high. And the best thing…his head was covered with the soft fuzz of new hair.

I learned a lot through him—a rough tough lad, no expressed sentimentality. To talk about 'love' just didn't fit. But having fun did. Ageless Spirit, true perception, sudden insight, showing me the joyful wickedness temporarily buried in his physical misery. For him, that was exactly the right way of 'letting go into love'.

And then the farmer, very different, although again presenting apparently a purely physical problem. A woman rang me one morning to say that her husband had put his back out and would I help? I watched him hobble up the mews, bent almost double, and it was with some difficulty that he climbed onto the couch. We had a half hour session, little spoken after the initial relaxation, and from my inner space I let energy flow up and down his spine, my hands gently resting where they wanted to go.

It was good to see him walk away upright again, but the following morning his wife rang back. 'He was absolutely alright last night, but putting his socks on this morning it went again. Can he come back?' I was reluctant, slipping straight back to the old ego trip. Me, ego proud, thinking with fear, 'I can't.' No intuition, no openness to the Ageless Spirit flow. 'I think it would be better, this time, if he followed the doctor's advice and went to the physiotherapist. Let me know how it goes.' Feeling faintly guilty, I promptly forgot all about him.

Ten days later he himself rang. 'I've been back for physiotherapy, but it wasn't half as good as coming to you. Please can I come back?' This time it was different. I didn't know the man at all, and had no idea whether he would want or be able to cooperate. But my intuition said, 'Go ahead.'

So back he came, and when he was totally relaxed, face down, I told him I was laying a gold rope of energy down his spine, very fine, but immensely strong. 'I want you to imagine it holding your spine in place. Can you do that?' A long pause, but eventually a muttered, 'Yes.' Now I felt it was time to go further, his turn to welcome the healing energy. 'That's good. Now, will you allow something to come to mind that can be a healing symbol for you—a flower, a bird, a picture, anything you see is right for you. Don't think about it, just watch.'

There was a long silence this time. 'Have you got one?'

'Oh yes, I got it straight away. It's a flower, a bright yellow flower.' And he described it fully.

'Wonderful, just look at it, enjoy it, and know that while you are looking, healing is taking place. You yourself are allowing it.'

Gently, after a few minutes, I brought him back and he sat up.

'Now—homework. I want you to promise to spend a few minutes as soon as you get up, sitting looking at your flower, and the same before you go to bed. And at any time, when you are out on the farm, just bring it to mind and let it work for you. The other thing is your rope; in times of physical stress pull it out and let it snap back into place. If you need to lift something heavy, or bend, or twist, just be sure it is in place and holding you *firm.*'

This time, his walk down the mews was completely upright. I heard no more, but about two months later, shopping in the nearby market town, I saw him coming out of the supermarket carrying a huge box of groceries.

'Martin!' I said in dismay.

'What's wrong? Nothing the matter with *my* back!'

So physical, and yet at the same time, such a keen connection had been made at intuitive level. He was whole.

There was the woman who was two stone overweight. Her son was getting married in the summer and she was dismayed at the thought of the inevitable wedding photos showing up this flabby woman.

'Will you help me lose weight?'

'I don't specifically do that. Let's just see what you need in your life.'

Over the next few weeks we explored this life. I gave her exercises to do. In one she had to imagine her ideal, beautiful, spiritually centred self, in actual detail of body language, clothes and expression, then allow herself, today, to merge with that self and experience its stance and creativity. Gradually she began to discover her strengths, actually to approve of and be kind to herself, see her value as a person. She came fortnightly and I said she should not go near her scales, except on the morning of the visit.

On the second visit she looked bemused. 'I've lost half a stone,' she said, 'but I haven't dieted, nothing's different.

'Nothing?'

'Oh, I *feel* different, but that won't make me any thinner.'

No comment, but on the next visit she began to see what was happening.

'It's easier now, when I'm doing the work you have given me, to blend with my ideal self. I can *be* that woman, I'm changing. And I'm busy in the evenings now—oh—I haven't needed to go to the biscuit tin.'

I found it exciting to see her bravely shed the coat of fat that had been her protection, and find the rather beautiful woman within. I never saw the wedding photos, but I'm almost certain she would have been wearing the outfit she bought in faith, shortly after she first came to me. 'It's two sizes too small, but I couldn't resist it.' Perfect.

I said earlier that we could anticipate joyful surprises in healing. One megga surprise came from working with a woman who had come a very long distance with the agonising pain of trigeminal neuralgia running up her face. The pain had been so bad that she had risked an operation on the nerve itself; it had failed, and she was desperate. She lay on the couch while I quieted us both and silently asked for help from the Source of all energy. I had only just begun the healing session, my hands held above her head, when her whole body gave an enormous jump. Startled, I hoped sounding confident, I asked her if she was alright, and then quietly continued, though I could see by her expression that something had changed. The pain had gone.

I can only think that in some way the remaining nerve had been trapped. This sudden movement, inspired by the Life itself, had freed the blockage. My prayer was answered, her ordeal was over, and we spent the rest of the hour being thankful together.

What about emotionally presenting problems? Does it really matter through which energy stream the problem presents? *All* of us are affected—one energy just urges us to look, and find a solution. Ultimately the cause may be elsewhere, and as the major trigger, needs itself to be dealt with later.

There was the lass who came for healing because she was so depressed she could no longer function properly. She was a painter and her creative ability had just vanished. She drudged along, day after day, submerged in a grey life fog. We didn't spend time talking, just got her comfortably relaxed on the bed, and I started to work through the colour scheme given me by Lily, my first tutor—specific colour to specific energy centre.

First, as always, the motive for her best good, and mine. But instead of the usual deep blue and gold for the head centre, I could see nothing but rose. The brow centre needed rose too, and the throat centre. I went on down…the heart centre also needed rose. In this system, rose is the colour of loving and I suddenly heard myself asking, 'Has your life been very short of love?'

She started to cry, and as I continued, soaking her centres, her organs, her tissues, her emotional and mental energy streams, every bit of her with rose, she quietly sobbed. It felt right. Finally we finished and I left her resting as I went to wash my hands. When I came back she got up, all cried out, but somehow lightened. I gave her a hug and sent her off. Three months later she wrote. She was living again.

Very different, and yet perhaps exactly the same, was the lass who, for fifteen months after shocking birth trauma had struggled with post-natal depression. Living in deep shadow, she endlessly berated herself for being so stupid! She was really ill and in the short time of her visit I had no hope of helping her in any major way. (Ah me, thinking-type expectation again.)

She had had a tape from me, but been unable to work with it to any great extent. Self-worth nil, she had been afraid of 'not getting it right'. We followed up one or two of the visualisations, but finally I just offered her half an hour healing. She leaned back in the big easy chair and I stood behind her. What did I do? Asked so much for her return to wholeness, worked on the energy round her head, then threw out any ideas of method. Following inner prompting, I just stood firmly holding her shoulders. Travelling in myself, I took her with me, Ageless Spirit, quietly repeating 'strength, strength, strength' as I felt the Ageless Spirit flow of strength and courage tingling through my fingertips. At the end I asked her how she felt? 'I don't want to leave,' she replied.

Her friends came to pick her up, bringing her little daughter, a gorgeous lively child, obviously adoring her mother. All through her depression, with her own mother's support, she had done so well to keep this child happy and safe, and I said so. For some reason I could not get her out of my mind, and after a few weeks dropped her a card saying I was thinking of her and hoped she was better. I was amazed to have a phone call saying everything had changed; she was back at work, and recovering fast. Wonderful.

The healing experience that taught me most, I think, was a sharing with a lovely woman dying of lung cancer. She was determined to live, and to spend an hour with her, experiencing her immense courage and rejoicing in the slight easing of breathing that followed, gave us both an enormous sense of peace.

She deteriorated fast and was finally admitted to the small local hospital, where oxygen and nursing support were available. I visited her in the evenings so that the relief gained might allow her a little sleep. In this case of desperate need any method seemed irrelevant. So far as I could I centred in, to my deepest place, and from there reached out to her.

A few days before she died I went in to find her struggling for breath and in huge discomfort. My prayer for her that night must have been an inner *shout!* I asked her, once again, if she wanted to live, for it seemed important that she always be given a chance to talk about death as well as life. Once again the answer was 'YES'. In reply I heard myself saying, 'I think you are too tired to fight for life any more. Life energy is indestructible, a natural healing force. All you need to do is to *trust* the Life-energy and go with it, wherever it takes you. Just allow.'

Then, as I stood beside her, sharing this energy, with every little puff of breath came the whisper 'allow'.

'You needn't *say* it,' I said, but she just smiled and continued. Gradually the breathing struggle slowed and I could settle her into bed.

Two days later I came in to find her, for the first time, emotionally distressed.

'What's the matter?' I asked.

'It's Daddy. He says that this is all for my best good, and we should talk about dying. I don't want to talk about dying, I want to live.'

'Alright, let's talk about living.' And to my surprise, for we had not done this before, I suggested, 'While I'm doing the healing, could you follow a guided fantasy? To pull in some energy?'

Such a commonplace visualisation, but that night so immensely powerful. She became a tree, a great strong tree, pulling up energy, through her roots, from the earth. Then we moved up, to feel the strong connecting energy of the trunk. At this point her hand came up and started waving about.

'What are you doing?'

'I'm adding life circles, like you see in a tree trunk.'

Finally, up to the high branches, energy down from the sky. Up went her hand again, better to pull it down. And her own energy did change, quieter, more relaxed, easier.

But I knew there was more. 'Could you follow another one? Be a tiny twig floating down the river, the Life river?'

I waited a few moments. By the expression on her face I could see how unpleasant this was.

'What's happening?' I asked softly.

'It's horrid. I'm getting tossed onto the rocks and the water's all over me. I can't breathe.'

And indeed, her breathing was difficult again. 'Remember, this is in your imagination. Change it, make a happy ending to the story.'

I didn't realise then what I was asking. Neither did she, but it was wonderful to watch. Her poor tired pathetic little face positively glowed.

'What's happened?' I asked.

'Oh,' she said, 'it's lovely. I've come out of the river and I'm lying in the meadow among the flowers.'

Out of the inner country had come her release as accurately and unknowingly she described her own death.

I kissed her and gave her a gentle hug. 'I'll be back on Monday, goodbye, my love.' But as I drove home I suddenly knew she would not need to wait till Monday. She died quietly the following day. She was in the meadow.

When her husband rang to tell me, and to thank me because she had so much needed what I had to share with her, I told him how very much she had given me. And I said how sorry I was that in this case healing had not meant curing symptoms.

'Oh,' he said, 'healing isn't about symptoms, it's about knowledge.'

This from a man who had said on my first visit, that he knew nothing about healing!

I've tried, then, to give you a picture of many different parcels of skin and bone, many different problems to be solved, presented as requests for healing. And each, in his or her different way needed only one thing, to be re-introduced consciously to inner energy, to feel again part of the Love of the Ageless Spirit.

It isn't, of course, all happy storybook endings. Duality is always beside us, around us, even within us. Maybe our mental energy, more often our emotional energy, begins to divert into tuned-out directions. Inevitably the mental, emotional, physical progression follows, and whoops, we are ill, sometimes in very subtle ways. But all life is one, and maybe at this point one of us (one of *you*), tuning in to the Centre, can take in with us the person-in-need. The wee mouse mauled by the cat busy with its outer life pursuits needed outer warmth and shelter, yes. But perhaps even more it needed the inner country energy of flowers, presented through Rescue Remedy, and those of my inner connection, presented as love, concern, and trust.

What about the people who know nothing of the spiritual life, or 'tuning in' or any of these theories? How can these ideas of healing apply to them? Simple. Everyone, all life forms 'know', but many still have to remember. The process is the same; sometimes the healing is more dramatic as light shines in. Go to any hospice and watch it at work. And so you see that healing, as with Claire, is not about symptoms, though hopefully it may be. It is about coming back to wholeness, accepting the great Love expressed through the Ageless Spirit. And as we saw in my few illustrations, though the Love itself may be constant and pure, the differing translations of it will be as many as the human beings receiving it.

So here we go. I say to you, as you read this, accept that you are a healer. Does this sound strange and frightening? Are you confused by the bigness and littleness of the concept? All I am asking you to do, every day, in meditation, in stillness, with anticipation, with trust, is to recognise your full potential. Increasingly to welcome and use your many life and Spirit connections: coincidence, intuition, openness, light. To become more friendly with the Ageless Spirit, of whom you are part. Healing is just sharing this friendship.

Throw out all the 'old age' limitations. 'I can't get about much.' 'I'm not into modern technology.' 'It's too late…'—you know the rest. I've told you about sitting in my patio sending out healing thoughts. Another good time is when you can't sleep at night. Use the other ways too—a smile in passing, a quiet demonstrated concern, a hug, a phone call…all manifestations of healing. Enjoy yourselves!

9

DAMS and DITCHES

But what about the days when you are the one who needs healing? It's raining when you wake up in the morning, prospect of a grey day. Or by contrast, it is beautifully hot and sunny and you don't at all feel part of it. Sometimes a very small thing throws you—a tone of voice or even a smile reminds you of times past, and grief wells up again. Or just no reason at all. The Ageless Spirit 'you' seems to have packed up and gone away, leaving the outer you lonely and deserted, and dark.

At these times it is almost impossible to meditate. Make the effort, calm down, quieten and immediately, like a scatter of busy mice, thoughts start to scamper all over and squeak for attention. Calm yourself, in again, and back they come. I remember very well when standing in a cathedral bookshop, devouring books as fast as I could, coming across a book by the then Dean of Westminster. It was the story of a year of ME in his life. 'The worst thing,' he said, 'was that I couldn't pray. Other people had to pray for me.' I found this a real relief—it's not just me!

In practical terms, at such times, when be-ing is too hard, I always fall back on doing. A walk in the country, a light book (serious ones tend to bring back the mice!), a scented bath, phone call to a loved friend…Anything that affirms my now submerged identity, reassures me that I'm OK and not alone in the temporary slip into one of life's ditches.

The other resource is the magic 'as if'. Did you realise that your unconscious is a yes-man/woman? Believes and acts on the messages you pass on to it. A young lass saying, 'I'd love to have a partner, someone kind and strong, and funny.' 'YES,' says the unconscious, and the message goes out on the life-telegraph. 'But someone like that probably wouldn't like me, I'm not good enough really.' 'YES,' says the unconscious again, the message is lost. We've talked already about self-worth, finding out more about the person you were born to be, even calling in your special-to-love child for re-enforcement. Now is the time for lots of positive messages for your personal yes-person, 'as if' they were true (they are) and you believed them.

But deep in a ditch (of your own making, though it may not seem that way), any resource seems out of reach or irrelevant. 'It's all rubbish anyway,' and you sink further into the mud. Some of these ditches are stuffed with chocolate, biscuits, cream cake, and fill you up with comfort eating. Some are soft and oozy and send you to bury yourself in bed, pull the covers over your head, and opt out. You will know others.

Yet every single ditch has a tiny escape ladder, with the magic 'as if' shining from it. Out you come, and just pretend you are back in the Ageless Spirit flow—'as if'…It won't feel like it, not at first, but gradually your unconscious will get the message and energies will change. Stand tall and straight 'as if' you felt brave and strong and ready for anything. It actually is very hard to curl up in a ditch of misery when your physical body is saying the opposite. Do the giving part of a healing message 'as if' that was how you felt. Smile at a miserable face in the street 'as if' you had joy to share.

Do you see how it works? We are made up just of energy, and if we change the direction of our personal flow, even by just pretending 'as if', then almost certainly it will alter. Try it—find your own way of climbing out of today's particular ditch 'as if' it were obvious and easy. And if by any chance a strand of emotional energy says 'But I can't, or I don't, or I feel…' turn it round quickly, challenge it. 'You are not me, you are just some of my energy. And I am moving in this or that direction now, even if you, my emotions, are not supporting me yet. But do come with me.' And if you are patient and can trust the magic of the 'as if' directive, then sooner or later, they will.

Those are the ditches—what about the dams? It seems that over our long lives we have kept on adding boulders to the dams that we allow to impede the Ageless Spirit flow. Here it is, flowing all round and within us, our very Being, and yet, adamantly it seems, we have kept on saying no, and holding it back, semi-permanently blocking in some areas. We have never stopped it, of course. How can you stop the Life-Love flow? But instead of the openness, the passion, the beauty, the love, at times we have only allowed a trickle to get through here and there. Small channels to keep reminding us of who we really are, of who we were born to be.

What if there were no dams—yours, mine, theirs? What if the Ageless Spirit flowed free, inner life directing, supporting, enhancing, shining through all outer actions? Can you imagine a universe flowing with love, respect for life, creativity, growth, growth, growth? No terrorism, no terrified retaliation, no hurting of any life form?

Right now, in your everyday aging life, you can choose to be an important practical illustrator of this dream. Look at just one Ageless Spirit quality to see what I mean. Take the concept of peace. We tend to think of peace as the opposite of war, as an international aim, as a big shining resolution. But big things start small. How peaceful is your home, your life, are your thoughts, your emotional currents? If you and you and you—and me—could live a truly peaceful life in all the small everyday things, and they and they and they could do the same, then that energy, cherished and maintained, eventually would reach flashpoint, like the hundredth monkey, and there would be peace. Lots of small, one huge.

Each year, in early June, I make a point of going for a walk in protected meadows, a few miles away. No weedkillers, no artificial fertilisers, and there before you is this amazing riot of wild flowers, amid long grass as the hay is left to grow. Buttercup, clover, Queen Anne's lace, cross-wort, speedwell, stitchwort, cranesbill, a gently moving magic carpet of yellow and white, with an occasional blue, pink, or purple. To me it feels like an offering to God—only presented for a couple of weeks, but almost shouting the presence of the Ageless Spirit. And you might notice, in passing, that one bit of clover isn't much to look at, one buttercup, one stem of swaying grass. It is *together* that the magic sings. And I'm saying to you, don't ever see yourself as just one old person, plodding on in the spiritual journey, not consistent, not, you may feel, very good at it, not strong enough now to make a mark or offer adequate help. Yes, agreed, you are just one buttercup, but there would not be the whole field if you and you and you did not grow together. The very fact of be-ing, of meditating, of steadily growing, of saying 'YES' to the Ageless Spirit makes an offering to God, or source, and at the same time, within the whole field, a vast offering to humanity around you. Believe it, and keep plodding.

Does this sound too high falutin', too idealistic? I hope not—let's look more closely at some of these boulders. What dams have you built in your life, to hold back the Ageless Spirit flow? Obvious boulders, like anger, and beside it, propping it up, fear. These two are so closely related. Usually we are angry *because* we are afraid. Someone is intruding in our space, someone is hurting, or threatening us, or our children, or friends, or nations. Or so often, our property or physical boundaries. Afraid, we fight back in anger.

Another nasty little boulder, quite small, but sharp, is the fear of failure. This crops up even in the spiritual journey. 'I'm not good enough,' 'I can't do it properly' (where has the be-ing vanished?)! 'Compared with him or her, I haven't the certainty'—and so on.

Another rough cracked rock is lack of forgiveness, especially for yourself. Old age gives plenty of time to look back at life mistakes...usually forgetting how apparently miserable outcomes may sometimes have ruthlessly opened up new growth patterns? Worry, anxiety, stress, lack of trust, all build up in a kind of miserable sludge that hardens into another boulder. Grief, held onto for many years, makes watery channels that divide and divert the Ageless Spirit flow. And you know the rest.

Old age, I think, causes many to suffer from the same old anger, worry, fear paralyses as do the young, but the emphases probably change. Physical, sometimes mental problems, arise, bringing fear of vulnerability, dread of future incarceration, all sorts of diminishing health problems for self or partner. Loneliness, common to all ages, bites hard among older folk who may have lived many years in loving company and suddenly have to travel solo. And, as we have already noted, the very fact of aging causes many relationships to vanish.

Dismal picture, isn't it? And one that many of us get stuck in. So I want you to look at it differently. Here's a resource for these dammed up times. When you have read it, be prepared to put this book down for a moment or two, make yourself as relaxed and comfortable as you can, close your eyes and be ready to travel on a route I am suggesting. You may like to tape the whole story—it is in two sections—but once it is familiar you will have no difficulty in just travelling under your own steam, so to speak.

◆   ◆   ◆

Picture a most beautiful river. It is flowing through lovely quiet countryside. Flowers in the meadows, trees bending lovingly over the water, birds almost skimming the water, chasing flies.

◆   ◆   ◆

Perhaps you are sitting on a rock nearby. If it is a hot day your feet may be in the water, which is making cool circles and eddies around you before it flows on. Just go into the peace of the scene, feel the sun, hear the birds and be still.

◆   ◆   ◆

You belong here, you are welcomed, for this is the Ageless Spirit of which you are part. It is flowing, totally unobstructed. For a little while sit quietly, eyes closed, and BE it. You are in the flow.

♦   ♦   ♦

When you are ready, quietly stretch, open your eyes, and come back, fully to continue your outer life. But bring that strength with you!

Use this resource at times when you feel you are travelling alone, no knowledge, no vision, just a weary isolation. The Ageless Spirit is temporarily out of your sight, you feel trapped in some sort of unsought diversion. Sit then, in peace, and watch the great river. And there is more. And some days you may want to travel further. Put yourself into your quiet relaxed space again, as nearly as you can, close your eyes and be ready to move on.

♦   ♦   ♦

As you start to wander further along the riverbank, you can see the places where in the past the water has overflowed. Was there a lake, or did the river just leave its proper channels and flood the countryside? Why?

♦   ♦   ♦

In your imagination you can see how rocks at that time steadily built up to make a dam. Not just your dam, everybody's dam, resisting, avoiding, fighting, losing the Love of the Ageless Spirit in troubled times. So what happened, what now? How has the river become again a secure and steady flow? Share the feeling of the dammed up river, and then the urgent need to free the flow. What can be done?

◆   ◆   ◆

Then watch, and see how it was tackled. The farmers came first, close to the earth and its needs, and afraid too for their livestock. With tractors and pulleys they heaved away some of the biggest boulders. Then work parties came to clean the river. Folk from all over the world, coming together, release trapped love, peace, joy, and spiritual knowledge. Quietly watch as the river is cleared.

◆   ◆   ◆

And that is not all, for in the distance you can hear the roar of a great waterfall as the river changes levels. Approaching, stand and watch. Thundering down, the water forces its way through a rocky channel at the top. It is beautiful. Great clouds of spray make rainbows in the sun. And down below the river settles again. First, as a wide spread of churning water, then, moving on as the smooth steady flow you have experienced above. Watch, and enjoy, for the dam has gone. Some of the boulders are still piled at the water's edge, but many, still in the river, washed and washed and washed by the fast flowing water are smooth now, and low, and make no obstruction.

◆   ◆   ◆

Stay with that picture as long as you need, then quietly, opening your eyes and stretching, come back, renewed.

And it seems to me that these pictures describe the two ways we can deal with the boulders blocking the river for us. Same idea, though a different metaphor this time, as that of a glass filled with dirty water. You want it filled with clean water, so what do you do? Either you tip out the dirty water and fill it up with clean, or you just direct a hose of clean water into the glass, and the dirt has to go, no room for it any more.

I think moving the boulders is like tipping out the dirt from the glass. You may well need to do this. Perhaps you need to find a good counsellor (remember the 'magic' requirement) or a good friend to share with, and ask for help. Or to follow a therapy programme of some sort, even one taken from a book or books. And gradually you may find you can put aside some of the emotional boulders, or find that they are now too small to cause obstruction. Even medication may at the right place, at the right time, be helpful to clear your river, empty your glass. No shame in that. And don't say, 'I'm too old, I can't go through all this, it's too late.' I tell you, it is never too late, and do you really not want to be a buttercup, fully flowering, weedless, shining in the sun, and adding to the magic carpet in the life-field—even for a short time, as they do?

And once again, where is your self-worth, and with that self-worth, the ability to say 'Yes, this is what I need' and not feel lessened thereby? It is so strange, our unkindness to ourselves. Even the need to move on in the spiritual journey can turn round to be a self-criticism. 'Right now, I just can't meditate, I fall asleep.'(So, I'm a failure.) Especially for us older folk discouragement on the journey often arises from genuine unmet physical needs. And these needs ask to be met first. Look at it in a more acute situation. If you were to visit a third-world country where people were starving, children could not be warmly clothed, had no shelter for cold nights, what would your priorities be? I can guarantee you would not gather folk round and say, 'What you most need is to learn to follow a spiritual path, trust, believe, follow your intuition.' You would be heating huge pans of soup, sorting out bundles of clothing, organising primitive night shelters. Practical down to earth priorities, but at the same time the most spiritually expressed Ageless Spirit Love.

The same applies to you, especially if you are on your own and must do it for yourself. Physical comfort, help with pain, adequate sleep, and cheeringly simple physical nourishment, all these can be found and enjoyed within a completely spiritual energy. Too many people think of the spiritual life as being exclusive. It is not—it is inclusive.

So that is tipping out the dirty water, putting aside the obstructive boulders method, on our own, or with other people.

What about the other way? The force of water from a hose flushing out the grubbiness…The force of a river in spate, smoothing jagged edges, widening cracks and making quiet channels. How do I use that way? It's all about seeing from a different angle, about coming forward with a huge steady support, about approaching from the opposite end, the Ageless Spirit end! In the first way we set out to clear the boulders so as to be in free flow for the spiritual journey. This way we *use* the free flow, in trust, to build differently.

I read a lovely description of a way to use this second method. Imagine a very stained tea towel that you rinse out in clear water. The stain diminishes, so you rinse it again. Still less, so again and again till the towel is quite clean. I have not been following this method for long, but find it works: The Ageless Spirit is there, a clear rinse, willing and able to absorb whatever would obstruct your access to the flow.

In practical terms, what exactly do you do? I find that I decide, in my mind, which most needs to change, boulder on my journey.

Quite simply, before meditating, I set this up as a firm intention a goal for which I need help. Then I completely let it go, no thinking about it, to strengthen the possible objections, no blurring of the original statement. Just quiet meditation underlined by 'joyful anticipation'. Again, I need to remember it is completely open anticipation. I don't know what will happen, or when, or how. No definite expectation to cause barriers.

Soon after learning about this type of dam-busting, I had startling evidence of its efficacy. New neighbours in the adjoining cottage have changed my lifestyle considerably. Very wealthy, very power seeking, very materialistic, they bought a charming wee cottage and are putting all effort and huge amounts of money into turning it into a luxury small town house! The problem for me is their love of noise. When they first came, the noise of Radio One was loud enough to penetrate our very thick stone walls with a high pitched whine, laced with chattery voices. But the really intrusive noise comes from a little Black and Decker workbench, erected on their patio, up against mine, only divided by a low stone wall. Roughly six or eight feet away sits my garden chair, but every day there is some sort of machinery noise, hammering, drilling, sawing for the latest little alteration. If I take refuge inside, then the results of the hammering follow me in.

My non-judgemental spiritual directives are strained. For me, quiet is a necessity. I find it vastly difficult never to know if I may be able to meditate, to rest, to enjoy the garden. Thankfully I do get occasional breaks when their 'large detached house, bees, veg., wonderful garden, five layered water feature…' draws them home.

What to do? Move house seemed to be the obvious answer, but now I wonder. One lunchtime, workbench deserted for lunch break, it seemed to me that a very firm inner directive said to me, 'Go out into the garden, settle into your chair, and meditate.' I did what I was told, holding in my mind, offering for solution the problem of coping with this noise. As I sat down and closed my eyes, instantly—no preparation, no breathing, etc.—I was deep in my meditation space. A huge sense of peace settled round me and for an hour I didn't open my eyes.

I presume it would be about ten minutes later when they came out. I didn't know what they were doing, lots of to and fro-ing and thumping, creaking of polythene sacks, etc. But it didn't matter, it didn't disturb me, and it was a weird feeling, meditation, quiet, peace with me, and just over the wall thumps and bangs and loud voices. They might well have been half a mile away. I only jumped once when the woman banged down the metal lid of their bin, but straight away I was back in. They finished before I did and there was a happy corollary. Apparently they had been doing a big clear up before going away for a couple of months. All was very well. Now, of course, I have to hold on to trust and try not to build a boulder of dread for their return

So experience this way of breaking up your dam. And it is not effort, not willpower, not trying, just offering to the Universe your need and, with joyful anticipation and trust going in, time after time, then to wait and see what and when and how are the results.

This is not meant to be a book solely of resources. There are many of these, visualisations, exercises, directions, and the right one will always come your way, if you stay open and allow. You may want to use candles, crystals, aromatherapy, whatever is right for you. I love to visit the big bookshop in our nearest town and browse in the Mind, Body, Spirit section. Blessings, they have started a coffee bar, with lovely big squashy sofas to collapse into as you dip into whatever is your latest find.

But I hope you have found things here that, as Quakers say, will 'speak to your condition'. In the last chapter I'm going to look at some of the ways we can make the spiritual journey stronger, safer, and, oh yes, adventurous and exciting. Never ever think that you are too old for a bit of fun, a bit of a risk, more adventuring. Pick up your stick, if you need to, but get going.

10

STILLNESS

For me, all the adventuring starts with stillness. How do I reach stillness? How do I know I have found it? Is it true that as I travel, stillness is the first gate I must open on the spiritual journey?

I have found stillness in many places, often unexpected and deep. Sometimes it has been at the end of a lengthy search, but sometimes a gift I only need to accept; a high tide softly sucking at the sea wall as it sways to and fro in the dusk; a summer day in the woods, gentle breeze encouraging every tree in a different dance movement, with awesome choreography; early pre-dawn in a country garden, silence broken only by the plaintive bleat of a wandering lamb; togetherness after a loving sexual relationship; huge peace and comfort sometimes just flowing in after a tempestuous release of grief and tears.

Always, I think, stillness is encompassing. I cannot find it, know it, unless I enter it. And I cannot fully describe it, for it is not worded. Many of you will have experienced this true stillness, often in brief flashes of time, sometimes as a longer gift. To hold it is to lose it. This is not effort, rules, conditions. It is pure being, in the stillness, you ARE. Don't try, just allow and welcome it. In it accept the Ageless Spirit holding.

Let's go further now. From the stillness, let's pack our travel bags with the things we will need on this particular life-stage of the journey. Qualities, beliefs, understanding, trust to keep us steady, strong and joyful, as we continue to learn and grow. Exciting, isn't it, as we manage travel with a freely changing outlook, just living in the now and welcoming adventure to come. And again, this is not asking for effort, or tiring cooperation. It is learning to accept and appreciate a very different point of view, working as Ageless Spirit, putting the magic into the ordinary. And enjoying it!

So what are we taking with us for this stage of the journey? Many of the bits and pieces we have mentioned already: true perception, open-ness, self-worth, vulnerability. But to me, the most important piece of baggage is simply meditation. And what does that mean?

Well, first of all, it means commitment. If I can meditate every day I am making a statement. I am saying, 'It is my clear intention to travel on the inner path.' And it seems that to do this I really need regularly to go in—to the place I call my meditation space. For there inner and outer merge, and I can experience something of the Unity that is Life.

This Unity has no barriers, so approaching it is not confined by rules and regulations. I do not, for example *have* to sit straight and follow specific instructions. I find myself in the meditation space in many different situations. Perhaps I am working deeply with a client, channelling healing. We go in together. Perhaps I am taking the dog for a walk at night, the moon floats still and silent above us, and the sense of unity is almost overwhelming. Perhaps I am listening intensely, wholly, to another person, with an open heart. Ageless Spirit moves in, and takes us both to the meditation space.

What is this space? It is a place of different expanded awareness. It is always there, but I do not always visit it. But I need a daily visit, a necessary quieting. Perhaps I can go in by first just watching my breathing, perhaps with a mantra, perhaps following an intellect-led exercise to soul and spirit, perhaps 'imagining'. All quite different, but also absolutely the same—the space is waiting for me, for you.

If you feel you need more definitive direction, or even a change of method, then do as I have suggested before, go to a bookshop, or the library, and see which book jumps out at you. You may not even need to do that, for if the need is recognised, then 'coincidence' may well produce it, just like that.

And as I've said all along, this can sound so easy and straightforward, and of course, it can be. But very often we get trapped, yet again, by feelings. Meditation is not about the feeling energy. It is really important to recognise this and be prepared to go beyond the emotional level. Some days, even weeks, meditation feels to be just an arid exercise. No good uplifting feelings, no great insights. So what do we do next? Make excuses. I'm too tired today, or too hot, or too cold, or not very well. Do you recognise these? We are told, too, that the nearer we are to a point of change, the greater the resistance. And we are so inventive, especially now when many excuses no longer fit. We don't have a big family to deal with, we don't have to take the children to school, we aren't too busy, with a pile of work to get through this evening. We don't even have to get up early and get on. I've elaborated here because I certainly have found that old age is a great age for avoidance. My favourite excuse for no morning meditation is realising around lunchtime, 'I forgot!'

But suppose we do manage to make a commitment and most days do meditate, persevering even when dryness creeps in. A more subtle avoidance may follow. During meditation we get a wonderful idea for a current project, or a lovely insight regarding a difficult relationship. And what happens? We forget all about the meditation and get carried away by the idea or insight. But not during your centring time, which is your precious time of growth, and as you persist, may eventually provide its own focus. As one writer puts it, leading you into the silent gap between thoughts.

For it is thoughts that, for most of us, refuse to lie down. And of course, the more we pay attention to the intrusion, the more they persist. It reminds me of a time, some years ago, when I lived in a little cottage at the end of a mews. There was a big flat stone step before my front door, and several of the small children who could play safely in the mews found it an ideal stopping place. Inside, I could hear the small high voices laughing and chatting, with occasional squabbling. Lots of jumping up and down, coming and going. I liked them there. Once in a while I had to rush out and kiss better some small person's battered knee, but on the whole I ignored them. I knew they were there, could hear them fairly clearly, but they were busy with their own lives, none of my business, and didn't disturb me at all. That, I think, is how we need to learn to deal with our 'thought children' during meditation, chattering, jumping up and down, busy, busy, busy. But none of my business. I hear them, and let them go. Try it—it works.

We have looked at difficulties in meditation. What about the benefits? So many—I find for me, just now that meditation is like 'going home'. If I am stressed and anxious, I take time out, settle down in stillness, as near as I can, focus and go in. At one point, I remember, I used to imagine a huge hand held out to welcome me. After ten or fifteen minutes, or even half an hour, I come back feeling washed and clean, and strengthened for whatever. And do remember, every time you go in, you are touching the unity of all life, you are part of the great Love that created the world, *is* the world. You have access to potential and wholeness beyond our everyday understanding. You ARE Ageless Spirit.

So this is a gift you can give yourself, and, because all life is energy, inevitably a gift you will share with those around you. Not words, just be-ing. And I'll let you into a secret: as I said before, you needn't follow the conventional meditation rules and posture. Sometimes it is lovely, tucked up cosily in bed, to 'go home' to say goodnight. And if, as you meditate in the night stillness, an angel comes along and whips you into sleep, so much the better—it's part of the gift.

That's the major baggage, then—so what else? In a rather odd way, the next small collection is to do with freedom. In my university days my philosophy tutor had written a book about freedom. The point he emphasised was that freedom had two sides—'freedom from' and 'freedom for'. You want so badly to escape from something, to be free. Why? Sometimes just the escape, and the result is not quite what you expected. Sometimes you have a steady goal in mind, and need to be free, to reach it. See the difference? When we look at freedom here, we are seeing the whole thing, both sides coming together as is always essentially the case when spiritually journeying. The freedom *from* is almost always leaving behind the *outer* chains we, or others, bound us with as life goes on. Freedom *for* is the increasingly uncluttered path to the inner stillness.

What are your chains? One of the heaviest fetters for older folk comes from a long lifetime of habit. We don't always think about our actions, thoughts or feelings. They are familiar and just happen. Reading a suggestion that judgement may be a hold-up in the inner life, I was startled to discover this habit in me. How very judgemental I had become! Assessing everything, good or bad, right or wrong—labelling, classifying, analysing, criticising, not least in relation to myself. How much energy was wasted there, busy busy, an almost endless intrusion on stillness. How to stop? Aha, and the answer is to be gentle. Set out to spend an hour, even ten minutes, not judging. Practise through the day, keep reminding yourself not to judge. Can you see freedom both from and for in this? So, go into the stillness, understand, and pack in non-judgement.

The next package may seem easier—just giving. The Ageless Spirit is waiting for you to be free. But as long as you grimly and fixedly hang onto possessions, people, even ideas, how can the Life Energy freely flow? Often, as older people, we may feel (and are told) that we have nothing much left to give. But life is made up of giving and receiving, as we said before, both sides of the same energy. If we don't let it flow, then we are stopping the circulation of life itself, a massive fetter.

In practical terms, what can we give, and how? Gifts don't have to cost money. The greatest gifts are energised from the inner space. Love, caring, appreciation, compassion, even, in some cases, wholehearted attention. And they don't have to be spoken; we talked about this in our exploration of relationship. Sometimes when I pass someone on the street who looks sad, miserable and alone, I silently send them the energy of hope, comfort and happiness. For someone who is angry, a beam of inner stillness. This silent giving is powerful, it can be a chosen habit silently to wish anyone you see 'Love, joy, and happiness'. I love doing this as I sit in the bus and mentally make my way down the aisle.

And of course, giving means receiving. What goes out must come in. So when I pack these giving qualities I not only commit myself to taking a gift whenever I visit someone—one flower, a funny story, a prayer, a compliment—I also remind myself to notice and be glad as I receive all the gifts life offers me today. The very young fluffy sparrow hopping fearlessly along my wall, the new rose in the garden, my large fluffy cat coming in through the bedroom window each morning and insisting on a loud purry love-in before descending to the kitchen for food. Taking the dog for an early evening walk and being surprised by a great scatter of absolutely minute baby wrens, zipping from bush to tree to wall, sharing their joyful energy of 'I am alive, I am out, I can *fly*.' Wow.

So again, enjoy the stillness, understand, and pack *giving*. Beside it put *conscious choice*. We've already noticed the chain of habit and this moves further into a kind of predictable behaviour reaction, a conditioning. We react in certain ways to stimuli in the environment, to people or circumstance apparently automatically. In actuality we are still making choices, just unconscious ones. And our choice usually rests on emotional currents.

Say that a woman goes to a party wearing delicate strappy sandals. Then a man treads on her foot. Quickly and unconsciously, she chooses to be angry and swings round to tell him off. Then she discovers he is blind and now chooses to apologise for *her* clumsiness. Later in the evening she sees him chatting and laughing, no more blind than she is—and chooses to be furious at his deception. But all that has actually happened has been a man treading on her toes, three unconscious choices.

So if at the moment of reaction, the moment of unconscious choice you can step back, witness, and make the choice a conscious one, then the power is yours, and the chain of habit and conditioning has to fall off. And just as giving-receiving needed to flow through heart love, Ageless Spirit Love, so choices need to be made in that energy. Ask yourself what the consequences of the choice will be, and then, will it bring happiness to me and to those who will be affected by it? If no, then that is not the choice. If in doubt, listen, rest in the stillness and feel the possible decision in your heart. If right, press on, if uncomfortable, wait, and check again, innerly, what the consequences might be.

Perhaps this is a new idea for you, but freedom from unconscious conditioning is another chain loosened, to allow you more and more to walk and move in the way of stillness, giving, loving and growing. So, from that place, pack conscious choice.

There is a lovely spiritual law called the law of least effort. A trio of attitudes add up to the attainment of this way of living: acceptance, responsibility, vulnerability—summed up as effortless ease. A slow steady-progress, without pressure, without constant trying to do this/that, attain this/that. But we find it hard to imagine living a life of effortless ease, don't we? For one thing, we find 'gradually' and 'slow and steady' such difficult concepts—we are always in a hurry. Even in old age we like to have a pattern of time and make sure that it is followed.

One of the ways to understand the rightness of this slow steady life progress is to spend some time just being quiet with nature. Natural life forces don't appear to be in a hurry; rather they adapt to fit their 'now', whatever that produces, in weather, changing conditions, even tragedy. In late Spring we watch the tips of bulbs appearing, and then a pause. After quite a long wait, especially if the weather is cold and wet, growth continues, shoots push up. But no hurry even then; eventually we see the green buds, extension almost of the stalks, and wait for them to tip over. And then, at last, they tip with just a hint of yellow. A few sunny days and this shining 'welcome to summer' flower lights our lives too. To watch, the whole process seems almost effortless, part of the flower's *now*, at each stage the plant just allowing, letting the life energy flow at its own pace, but finally a joyful blossom. Try it for yourself, be brave, live in the now, allow, pack the effortless ease, law of least effort. If this needs further exploration, let's look at the nature of different life forms growing towards wholeness. See how they allow the Life flow and prosper. It is the nature of flowers to bloom, of birds to sing, of sun to shine and stars to twinkle. They don't try, they just *be*, and do it. It is the nature of human beings to dream and trust and manifest the inner in the outer, easily and effortlessly, using the spiritual law of least effort. And so again, coming from the stillness, this is finding freedom, loosing the chains of so many old habits, like the need for control of others and the approval of others. Like the belief that money solves all problems, like the need for a sort of wearying chase of happiness, for focusing on the *outer* older person and his or her ego-enhancing qualities. Truly, these are heavy chains to be unloosed. Yet freedom is so simple. If your inner reference point is not ego, but Ageless Spirit, if needs come from the stillness, so that criticism is irrelevant, control unnecessary, then the wasteful chafing of the confining chain fades, and you are strengthened by the power of love.

Better still, you can move into that flow and, free, be able to facilitate not only your own progress, but contribute also to that of the universe around you. Ancient Spirit magic again. For as we experience freedom, things change. Unity with all life is the gift we experience. We learn to share love with all life forms. I keep a glass and postcard handy in the kitchen cupboard, ready to rescue any misguided fly, bee, or wasp who gets trapped on the inside of the window. People ask me what fertiliser I use to make my windowsill flowers so colourful and alive. When I say 'I just love them', they look at me with doubt, but it is true. I am so grateful for what they give me, and I need to tell them so.

Strangely, it isn't easy, this effortless way of living! It brings new lessons, especially the three I mentioned earlier. First, acceptance—I must accept the now of my life, believing that the whole pattern must be complete and good; I just can't see far enough yet to understand. Second, I must take responsibility for my situation, not always blaming everyone else, for I choose my reactions. And third, be brave enough to allow myself to be vulnerable, not always to be fighting for my point of view, recognising that from our limited perception there must be many points of view. And I must be on guard against chaining myself to any one of these.

So perhaps in the side pockets you should pack *acceptance, responsibility* and *vulnerability*. From the stillness understand the place of these three in the life of least effort.

Now travel further and pack *detachment*. I could not understand this at first. How can I love someone and at the same time practise detachment, impersonal and distant? I could not understand love as 'just' an energy. It seems odd to me now, as I recognise Love as the paramount life energy, with vast power and creativity.

I learned about it as an energy when, as a radionic practitioner, I was asked to treat a four-year-old Downs Syndrome boy. His life consisted of sitting on the floor all day, with a few toys around him, watching brightly coloured television. His Nana was his carer and took him on pushchair outings during which he beamed at everyone they met. But he couldn't walk, and leaked in all directions. Nana loved him to bits, which was just as well, as his parents had dis-owned him.

So I pulled out all the stops and treated him with every energy pattern in the book. No change. Coming downstairs one morning a voice inside my head said: 'Treat him just with "love" and fortify it with red.' I had never met this little boy, didn't therefore know him personally, so there was no outer dilution, just 'love'. Faithfully, for ten days, I blitzed him with love, on red.

On the tenth day, Nana busy in the scullery with the weekly wash, he crawled across the floor—first time ever—into the kitchen, and pushed the clotheshorse onto the fire! A dramatic start, and from there it was all go. That little boy learned to walk, to be dry and clean, and was later able to go to special school and continue his development. All through 'love'—a detached love.

Detachment comes from increasing belief in the power of your true Self. Take time, in your stillness, to appreciate this, for security follows this acceptance. Nothing can destroy the power of Ageless Spirit, working through and for you. If you digress and get chained again by attachment, then in a strange way, you exchange your trust and belief in Self, for symbols of this Self. Is it money that is power-ful and will make you secure? Of course it isn't—and of course it won't. People attached to money are often very insecure—it may vanish. All the things you build for security are actually attachment, to the known—your past, your unconscious choice conditioning. How can the life-flow break through that stagnation? Unless you detach from it and let go.

It's a case of taking a deep breath and accepting, even welcoming, *un*certainty. I think this particular step must rest very heavily on our sequence of 'stillness, joyful anticipation, trust'—all homing into the Self, the Ageless Spirit. Once you have taken it, then you are open to all sorts of wonderful possibilities. Throw away the rigid plan of what next and open your life, even now, at some level or other, to a whole range of as yet unknown possibilities. And, of course, you can have the intention of your life moving in certain directions, but within that intent other possibilities flourish. I have certainly found a huge release of tension in letting go of the need to force solutions to a problem. Do what I can, and then recognise the uncertainty and wait for the solution to happen. For every problem holds a gift, a chance, a new opening. If I can stay detached, don't force a quick 'secure' answer; then the resolution that *will* emerge can be surprising. Don't forget, now you are free and aware of being part of the great Life consciousness, possibilities are huge and can be exciting, fun, magic.

So what have we got in our baggage now—our immediate needs for the journey? Meditation, freedom, non-judgement, giving-receiving, life of least effort, detachment, uncertainty—what a heap! And of course, they are only packed for transport purposes. Take them out as you travel, use them, loose the chains and accept freedom.

Yet, in one sense, they could all be jettisoned. We could return, in total simplicity, to the stillness. For from here comes the life shift we need to make. From here too comes the courage to make it, the love to uphold us, and the trust to keep our beliefs steady enough to encompass our new discoveries.

Does all this seem too much? I have wanted so much, almost passionately, to share with you some of my discoveries in this life-stage of the inner journey. I feel so strongly the need to tell you that, far from being an older, tired, not very useful man/woman, you are potentially a powerful factor in changing the world. How? By connecting more and more with all the demonstrated aspects of Spirit, using magic, angels, healing. By walking proudly to the deathgate, joyfully anticipating the celebration there. And by frequently touching stillness and going through that, to the gap between thoughts, to the inner space from which you came, to which you will return, and which ceaselessly can provide nurture. Most of all, recognising yourself, with all life, as Ageless Spirit.

Keep journeying. Travel well.

978-0-595-39792-1
0-595-39792-1